SKY BLUE HEROES

SKY BLUE HEROES

THE INSIDE STORY OF COVENTRY CITY'S 1987 FA CUP WIN

STEVE PHELPS

pitch

First published by Pitch Publishing, 2015

Pitch Publishing
A2 Yeoman Gate
Yeoman Way
Durrington
BN13 3QZ
www.pitchpublishing.co.uk

A CIP catalogue record is available for this book from the British Library.

ISBN 978-178531-020-1

Typesetting and origination by Pitch Publishing

Printed by Bell & Bain, Glasgow

Contents

In life, if you're lucky enough to get into a situation where you are doing something, doing it well and loving what you are doing, you get a reward at the end of it which is the icing on the cake. We as professional footballers were plying our trade at Coventry City and we just happened to be in the right place at the right time. It was something that a lot of people strive for and not a lot of people get. For me, personally, we were very, very lucky, to be in that time and place. Playing for Coventry at Wembley in 1987 and throughout the cup run it was a great bunch of lads together and a great time for us all.

Brian Kilcline – January 2015

Acknowledgements

I WOULD like to thank all of the following for their goodwill, co-operation and willingness to contribute to this book. Thank you for taking my calls and replying to emails, these interviews were carried out between July 2014 and March 2015:

Steve Ogrizovic, Brian Borrows, Greg Downs, Lloyd McGrath, Brian Kilcline, Trevor Peake, Dave Bennett, Michael Gynn, David Phillips, Cyrille Regis, Keith Houchen, Nick Pickering, Steve Sedgley, Graham Rodger, Dean Emerson, Paul Culpin, Steve Cockrill, John Sillett, George Dalton, John Poynton, Graham Hover, Jenny Poole, Terry Gibson, Micky Adams and Chris Hughton.

John Motson, Neville Foulger, Stuart Linnell, Mike Liggins, Ian Woods, Rob Gurney, Steve Evans, Ian Bolton, Ian Winter, Bob Hall, Steve Lee, Gary Newbon, Alan Biggs, Andy Scaysbrook, Neil White and Steve and Heather Taylor.

Jim Brown, Andy Turner, Geoff Foster, Kev Monks, Mike Young, Dean Nelson, Matt Partridge, Matt Kerr, Blake Waugh, Danny Finlay, Moz Baker, Rob Summerfield, Calvin Urquhart, Lee Corden, Gavin Clifton, Frank Pritchard, Bob Eales and Neil Jones.

Lee Dixon and Jimmy Greaves for their contributions via Twitter – get well soon Jimmy.

Further thanks:

To the ever-patient Dave Bennett for ensuring I was able to speak with every player that brought FA Cup glory to the city of Coventry. Along with Cyrille, Dean Nelson and Steve Carpenter he also read through the first draft.

To Jim Brown and Mike Young at the Coventry City Former Players' Association, your assistance over the last year has been much appreciated.

Text acknowledgements: to the *Coventry* (formerly Evening) *Telegraph* for Neville Foulger's FA Cup Final match report and selection of articles written between January and May 1987 and to Jim Brown for his *Coventry City: The Elite Era – A Complete Record.* Thanks also to Robert Witts at the Herbert Art Gallery for use of their archives for my research.

Audio acknowledgements: John Motson for his BBC 1 FA Cup Final commentary and Stuart Linnell for Mercia Sound's semi-final coverage.

Photographic acknowledgements: Carl Newell – publications editor at CCFC. Thanks also to Graham Hover, Lee Corden, Rob Summerfield, Calvin Urquhart and Dean Nelson for their own personal photos.

Paul, Jane, Derek, Duncan, Dean and Gareth at Pitch Publishing.

To my wife Emma and our ten-year-old twin girls, Aimee and Jolie.

Finally, I never, ever thought I would write this line but a huge thank you to John Motson for his interview and foreword.

Steve Phelps

Foreword by John Motson

THERE are two things that stand out for me with the 1987 FA Cup Final. The quality of football was very high because I've commentated on a lot of cup finals where the game itself has been disappointing with quite a few 1-0 victories. It was very refreshing on the day as the two teams came out and played what I would call an open brand of football. There was no surprise in Tottenham doing that because David Pleat was the manager and they had been playing like that all season but Coventry were on a high by the very nature of the run they'd had and the fact they had got to Wembley in the first place. The way it ebbed and flowed it swayed from one team to the other and made it one of the best finals.

Clive Allen had scored well over 40 goals for Tottenham that season but when he scored there was a long way to go and Coventry got back into the game fairly quickly. The game moved on from there and I don't recall there being a break in the excitement, there was a great flow to the game. Wembley could be a bit of a furnace and it was a hot day. It was a bit unfortunate that the game was settled by an own goal but, nevertheless, I think at that stage Coventry were very much on top and becoming stronger as extra time progressed.

The feelgood factor that went around Wembley that day was hugely noticeable as, although Tottenham were on the losing side, they made a big contribution to the final as well as Coventry. The George Curtis–John Sillett partnership was the unique thing about the Coventry cup run, I can't recall the FA Cup being won by joint managers before, or after.

A big memory for me was my co-commentator Jimmy Hill's reaction at the final whistle because he made up his mind straight away that he would get the whole Coventry team up on to the BBC gantry at Wembley from where the two of us were commentating. Now, that's quite a long way away from the pitch and it involves lots of stairs and lifts but, I tell you what, he got them all up there and those interviews were conducted in the studio high above the pitch within half an hour of the game ending. No one else could have done that but Jimmy Hill.

Steve's collection of over 60 exclusive interviews, mine included, take you through season 1986/87 as the 'Cast of '87' are reunited for their first-hand recollections of Coventry City's greatest ever achievement in their long and proud history. This is a unique memory of a wonderful era and on that fabulous day at Wembley, 'The Sky Blues were sky high!'

Prologue

AN email from Pitch Publishing chief Paul Camillin landed in my inbox at the start of 2014, 'What about an '87 reflection book for 2015…Interviews with management, players, staff, fans and journalists?'

Having written *Coventry City On This Day* and *Coventry City Miscellany* with them, I knew Pitch realised that football extended beyond the Premier League. A 25th anniversary weekend was held in 2012 and *Coventry Observer* journalist Steve Carpenter teamed up with the Former Players' Association to speak with the players and publish a series of excellent articles in the paper. What had yet to happen was for the memories of many of those from 1986/87, not just the players, to be captured under one book cover.

A call to Jim Brown, the Sky Blues' club historian and statistician and chairman of the Former Players' Association, ensured I had their support. A call to Dave Bennett saw him speak to the playing squad about the book and then provide me with contact numbers. What hadn't been put in place was how to make contact with club staff of the time, board members, mascots, opposition players, club photographers, the teams from Mercia Sound, *Central News*, *Midlands Today*, *Coventry Evening Telegraph* and Radio WM. Where were the writers of 'Go For It City' and just who was that lad who jumped on to the pitchside photo at Wembley and where is he now, 28 years on? Wherever they all were, I needed to find them, while there was still time. And I did.

A Google search back in April 2014 found Mercia Sound's match commentator Mike Liggins at the BBC's *Look East* in Norwich while Mercia's pitchside reporter at Wembley, Ian Woods, was located, via Twitter, at Sky News. Mike and Ian were the first people I emailed and they replied immediately to confirm their participation. A day later it was the same with Rob Gurney and Stuart Linnell. The first player I spoke with was Cyrille, the last, back in March, was Brian Borrows. Each and every one of the players involved in the cup run gave me their time and it was great to hear their recollections of the season.

Between April 2014 and March 2015 I located and interviewed 62 people. The fans, some I know, some I've never met in my life, all had a story to tell of when Coventry and its football club united as one. I've watched the Sky Blues since 1979/80, I was 12 in 1987 and went to the Bolton, Stoke, Sheffield Wednesday and Tottenham ties, at that age you think you'll go back and win it again the following season.

I have not interviewed George Curtis as I was advised to not make contact due to health reasons. However, there are many warm anecdotes/tributes to George from many of those I spoke with which reflects the part he played in that wonderful season.

This book is written as a live timeline of the season as the 'Cast of '87' tell the story through their eyes as events unfolded on and off the pitch. In 1986/87 we all sang together.

The Cast of 1986/87

The squad: Steve Ogrizovic, Brian Borrows, Greg Downs, Lloyd McGrath, Brian Kilcline, Trevor Peake, Dave Bennett, David Phillips, Dean Emerson, Michael Gynn, Cyrille Regis, Keith Houchen, Nick Pickering, Steve Sedgley, Graham Rodger, Paul Culpin and Steve Cockrill.

The management team/club staff: John Sillett, George Dalton, John Poynton, Graham Hover and Jenny Poole.

The opposition: Terry Gibson, Lee Dixon, Micky Adams and Chris Hughton.

Mercia Sound: Stuart Linnell, Mike Liggins, Ian Woods, Rob Gurney and Ian Bolton.

Radio WM: Ian Winter/Ian Bolton.

BBC 1: John Motson.

Coventry Evening Telegraph: Neville Foulger and Steve Evans.

Central News: Bob Hall, Gary Newbon and Jimmy Greaves.

Midlands Today: Steve Lee.

Sheffield Wednesday matchday programme contributor: Alan Biggs.

Coventry City matchday photographer: Andy Scaysbrook.

'Go For It City' songwriters: Steve and Heather Taylor.

A selection of fans: Andy Turner, Geoff Foster, Jim Brown, Calvin Urquhart, Neil White, Dean Nelson, Mike Young, Kev Monks, Matt Partridge, Matt Kerr, Blake Waugh, Danny Finlay, Lee Corden, Rob Summerfield, Gavin Clifton, Neil Jones, Moz Baker, Bob Eales and Frank Pritchard.

JIM BROWN: In August 1986 I, like many City fans, wouldn't have believed that their team would have its best league campaign for almost ten years and nine months later lift the FA Cup at Wembley. Under the new managerial partnership of George Curtis and chief coach John Sillett the early weeks of the new season were heartening with an opening-day defeat at West Ham being followed by a seven-game unbeaten run which took the team to fourth place in the First Division table. Then, a couple of sloppy defeats reinforced the view that the form was a flash in the pan. What convinced me that the season was going to be something special was a hard-won home victory over Nottingham Forest in November. Brian Clough's team had always been a bogey side for the Sky Blues and would continue to be for several more years but John Sillett had done his homework and a Nick Pickering goal was enough to knock Forest off the top of the table. The new £40,000 signing from Rotherham, Dean Emerson, in only his fourth league game, was superb in midfield. The famous 4-3 victory over Tottenham at Christmas was unforgettable and reinforced my optimism of a top-six finish as we turned the corner into 1987...

LLOYD McGRATH: Dean and I complemented each other really well, he was a quality player. John signed him from Rotherham after we played them in the Littlewoods Cup. I was given a man-to-man marking role on him and he got the better of me, that's why he was signed. We were both different types of player but worked off each other well and made the midfield solid.

DEAN EMERSON: At Rotherham we played Coventry over two legs, late September and early October. We played well at Highfield Road in a 3-2 defeat and then in the return at Millmoor Brian Kilcline's header won it for them. A couple of weeks later Rotherham manager Norman Hunter told me Coventry had come in for me and asked if I would want to go. 'Of course I would' was my reply. They were in the top division and I signed straight away after meeting John and George. I made my debut on a Sunday against Wimbledon when we won 1-0 and six days later Oggy scored in the draw at Sheffield Wednesday.

NICK PICKERING: The penultimate game of 1985/86 was at home to Luton. We beat them 1-0 and I scored. It was a massive win, and then the last game against QPR we won 2-1 to ensure survival. George and John had taken over after I'd only been there for seven or eight games under Don Mackay and they brought Keith Houchen and David Phillips into the squad in pre-season. They had a chat with the older pros, Cyrille, Greg and Trevor. Cyrille was the main man, a fantastic player, a lot of people thought he liked the long ball but he didn't. He liked to spin and turn, he's not that big but a great athlete. I was on the left with Greg and Dave Bennett was on the right with Brian Borrows. It was into feet, spin, turn and cross it, you had a lad in Keith Houchen who was as brave as a lion.

BRIAN BORROWS: My first season at the club, 1985/86, was a tough one and then John took over from Don Mackay towards the end of the season. I couldn't have envisaged what happened in '86/87 with us reaching the cup final and having quite a comfortable season in the league. John simplified the playing style, it was get it to Cyrille who'd hold it up and we'd go from there. There was nothing complicated about it. John and George Curtis built a team spirit, we got momentum and the team had better players than people realised.

GREG DOWNS: When I first arrived at the club the management asked me to play a style I'd never played before. I'd left Norwich and John Bond after 11 years, renowned for playing good football, and was now whacking it long into the channels. I'd never played that way in my life and had a torrid time, my game was about overlapping and getting crosses in. George and John put the smiles back on our faces. 'Benno' showed what he'd got, Cyrille displayed his strength when the ball went into his feet and we knew it would stay there so I could overlap and bring Nick Pickering into the play. We had a team that could rise to situations and battle their way through. We were a bloody good team, we could knock the ball about and, when George and John took over, John had a chat with Cyrille and asked, 'How do you want the game played?' He replied, 'I want the ball to my feet.'

DAVE BENNETT: We had a bit of steel in the side, a squad with a sense of humour and a character that, if we weren't going to win the game, we weren't going to lose it. We were as good a team off the park as we were on it, doing well in the league and enjoying our football. From where we were the previous season to where we went, with the same group of players, to have a turnaround like that was remarkable. We were holding our own and not losing many games.

STEVE OGRIZOVIC: We had two people in charge, George and John, who were great at creating the right atmosphere within a football club making people feel good about playing for the club and it was all really enjoyable. The way they united the squad, we were quite a tight-knit group at that time, we still meet up now, that's the great thing about sport, the friendships that you form even though you don't see people for years on end but pick up from where you left off. We all have one thing in common — that great year of 1987. The Coventry fans are great, in adversity or success they turn out, we'd had a couple of relegation battles in years previous, Highfield Road was full in 1984/85, how we ever managed to stay up that year I don't know (we beat Stoke, Luton and champions Everton to stay up and relegate Norwich City). A lot of the players in those formative years had been bought by Bobby Gould and were getting better, more used to playing at the top level and improving. You could see the character and steely resolve in them having come through the Stoke, Luton and Everton games and 1985/86 saw us win on the final day to stay up too. We were improving and when it mattered we managed to produce results. It then all blossomed when George and John took over, we had a really good league campaign in 1986/87, confidence was high and everyone was gelling, starting to fulfil their footballing potential at the top level.

Coventry City Matchday Programme, Thursday 1 January 1987:

'Feet on the Ground' is the motto with which John Sillett will be aiming to improve on the high standards so successfully achieved by the Sky Blues up to the turn of the year. The chief coach says: 'We shall be looking to carry on the good work, the foundations for which we laid in the weeks up to Christmas. We know the history of recent seasons and we don't want the same thing to happen again. We have got a super draw at home to Bolton Wanderers in nine days' time and I am looking forward to it. The FA Cup gives you a little tingle more than any other competition. Hopefully we can do even better than we did in the Littlewoods Cup.'

As the city of Coventry welcomed 1987 to their hearts on a freezing cold New Year's Eve the first team squad were tucked up in bed to await the visit of John Moore's Luton Town. The Hatters were infamous for their artificial pitch and controversial ban on away supporters which led to their expulsion from the campaign's Littlewoods Cup. They restricted ground entry at Kenilworth Road to holders of a special membership card for which only home fans were eligible. Moore had been promoted from reserve team duties in the summer of 1986 to replace David Pleat who had departed for Tottenham Hotspur and they sat eighth in Division One as they visited Highfield Road.

The Sky Blues' 1-0 victory at Kenilworth Road the previous season saw them become the first visiting side to triumph on the artificial pitch which had no doubt contributed to Luton's ninth-place finish. Former Sky Blues Les Sealey and Ashley Grimes returned to take the points on a day when nothing went right for the Sky Blues. Brian Stein's low drive was enough to separate the sides as, on the final whistle, Sealey cartwheeled across the pitch to rile the City faithful as the jubilant visitors celebrated.

Two days later an even colder St James' Park, home of Newcastle United, welcomed City in front of 22,366 passionate, loyal Geordies. Dave Bennett and Cyrille Regis scored for the Sky Blues on a day made memorable by Brian Kilcline leading the side out of the dressing room... and into the car park! Once the laughter had subsided it was business as usual as the points returned to an only slightly warmer West Midlands.

With his goalscoring account for Coventry finally opened in the 4-3 victory over Tottenham, Keith Houchen looked forward to a brighter 1987. A pre-season injury, when he trod on a piece of glass, sidelined him for six weeks and left him behind the squad in terms of preparation, quickly followed by a stomach bug.

The Pink, Saturday 3 January 1987: Houchen: Year of hope

'After what I've gone through since the summer, things must get better in 1987. I suffered so many injuries I was beginning to think it wasn't meant to be. It reached a stage where I was almost frightened to knock on the treatment room door and physiotherapist George Dalton used to laugh when he saw me walk in. It was great to be back in the side for the Spurs game and even better to score a goal in such a tremendous match. The big thing is stopping in the team because there is such fierce competition for places. It is strange for me to have as few goals at this stage of the season. Normally, I have scored ten or 12 by Christmas but perhaps 1987 will be my year. I hope so.'

Across the country temperatures plummeted to leave training grounds treacherous and stadium pitches frozen. Not every club had undersoil heating and even this was no guarantee of a surface fit for professional football. With Ryton's training ground in no fit state for training, John Sillett and George Curtis took the squad away to warmer climes – Fuengirola, Spain. Bob Hall, then ITV's chief sports reporter in the Midlands, takes up the story, 'The winter of 1987 was very cold. Ice and snow prevented training and caused many postponements, so much so that when Coventry City found themselves drawn at home in the FA Cup to Bolton Wanderers on 10 January, their joint managers John Sillett and George Curtis decided a few days of warm weather was the perfect preparation, Spain to be exact.

'When news reached the sports desk at ITV in Birmingham, editor Jeff Farmer decided we should go too. I needed no second bidding and, together with a three-man crew (camera, lights and sound) headed for the Costa Del Sol. At Malaga airport we went to collect our booked hirecar, an estate, ideal for the gear, baggage and four of us. The girl on the desk apologised, "Senor, no car like that, we give you this instead." Her dazzling smile had me signing the documents in a flash.

'The vehicle was an 18-seater minibus, with column gear change. The crew and I stayed at the splendid five-star Don Carlos in Marbella, Coventry City stayed at the 2-star Los Pirameds in Fuengirola, the sort of concrete tower hotel you saw in Cosmos and Horizon holiday brochures of the time. I mention this only to explain why, what happened next, happened.

'We had arranged to go to the team hotel at 9am the following morning to film training. John Sillett was waiting at the hotel door for me, "Robert – good morning – have you heard of a health spa nearby called Byblos?" I confessed I hadn't so he took the crew to the beach to film training and dispatched me to "sort it out and see if we can all go for the afternoon". Byblos guest relations soon, sensing publicity, granted us use of the facilities. As I approached "Schnoz" (I had my ITV colleague and one-time team-mate of John at Chelsea, Jimmy Greaves, to thank for my knowledge of John's Chelsea nickname) with the good news he was smiling, "I knew you could do it, see you at 12.30 for lunch after training, be our guest, oh and in return, you can take us all there." It transpired the film crew had told John about our minibus and he had worked out we could all get in the minibus – and I could drive them.

'"Look at it this way, Robert, you're in a posh hotel getting access to all this so it's the least you can do." I nodded in agreement.

'What I hadn't realised was just how far up a mountainside this place was, how bad the road was, how difficult the drive would be or how uncomplimentary the players would be about my driving. The rest of the trip was excellent and the bond established.'

////////////////

As the build-up continued to the third round clash, Bolton player-manager Phil Neal gave his thoughts on the tie and task his side faced:

Coventry Evening Telegraph, Thursday 8 January 1987:

'Nothing to fear' Bolton boss Neal tells players

'I spotted one or two weaknesses in their armour [referring to the 2-2 draw at Highfield Road with Manchester City on 21 December]. I was impressed by the Coventry playing style but have told my players they have nothing to fear when they visit Highfield Road. The pressure is on Coventry to come out and win the game and, hopefully, it will become a test of footballing ability. That's what we like. We have put in a lot of hard work this week on sorting out what has gone wrong in recent matches and I think we have come up with the answer.'

For Sky Blues right-back Brian Borrows the tie pitted him against his former club:

Borrows: My old club will raise their game

'It's not going to be easy and if we start thinking it is we could be in trouble. For Bolton the match will be their cup final and they'll be giving it everything they have. There is no real pressure on them because no-one expects them to win. I'm sure we have the ability to do well in the competition but you have to rely on a spot of good fortune as well. But if we do have the luck of the draw I fancy our chances.'

Bolton were expected to bring 1,000 supporters to Highfield Road as City projected a crowd of around 12,000. Despite the widespread frost they were unable to switch on the undersoil heating as a fault in the boiler in the run-up to the fixture caused a series of bursts in pipes laid nine inches below the surface and any repairs would need to wait until the season's end. The undersoil heating system cost £40,000 when it was laid back in 1980 and City were one of the first clubs to install it. Along with Coventry, Manchester United's system had also recently failed.

One of the highlights for a young supporter is to fulfil the role of mascot. To lead the side out on to the pitch with their heroes is a memory no one can take away from them. Calvin Urquhart was selected as one of the two Sky Blues mascots for the visit of Bolton and says, 'Further to a phonecall from the club requiring confirmation that I had the kit (as they no longer supplied this) the letter arrived stating I was to be the mascot for my beloved Coventry City Football Club. This was to be the mascot for the FA Cup third round against Bolton Wanderers – being honest, I was gutted it wasn't one of the "big boys from the First Division" as they were in the Third Division at the time.

'I went to the Main Stand reception and it was all very informal. We were led to a small side room which wasn't the experience that I had in mind. However, due to my excitement this was quickly overlooked while getting changed into my replica kit made by Triple Sports (I still have the shirt to this day as a memento). I was then told by club officials to wait by the entrance to the tunnel and watch the players finish off their warm-up prior to the final team talk before I could lead them out on to the hallowed turf (well, it was in my eyes, anyway!). I had dreamt of being on this pitch while watching the team from my season ticket seat in the Sky Blue Stand. My nerves were starting due to having just asked my hero, "Big Cyrille", as he left the pitch for his autograph, of which he was happy to oblige.

'Suddenly, "Killer" appeared from nowhere and said, "Right lads, come on, let's go!" Bolton had already gone out first and they went towards the West End. I thought to myself, "You can't do that, that's City's end!" During the warm-up I had a kickabout with Dave Bennett and I was also waving to my dad's friend who was standing on the Kop. We then went to the centre circle to meet the opposition captain, Asa Hartford, for the coin toss and pre-match pictures. The referee asked us to leave the field of play as the match was due to commence.'

City: Steve Ogrizovic; Brian Borrows, Brian Kilcline, Trevor Peake, Greg Downs; Michael Gynn, David Phillips, Dean Emerson, Nick Pickering; Cyrille Regis, Dave Bennett. Subs: Steve Sedgley, Keith Houchen.

Bolton: Mike Salmon; Derek Scott, Mark Came, Dave Sutton, Jimmy Phillips; Asa Hartford, Julian Darby, Warren Joyce, Mark Gavin; Steve Thompson, Tony Caldwell. Subs: George Oghani, Mark Winstanley.

Referee: Mark Scott.

The Pink, Saturday 10 January 1987: Nice 'n' easy! Gynn stars as City stroll it Coventry City 3 Bolton Wanderers 0 (Downs 15, Regis 18, Bennett 45) Att: 12,051

Take-it-easy City cruised through into the fourth round of the FA Cup at Highfield Road today in front of 12,051 supporters. They booked their place at the expense of Bolton with first-half goals from Greg Downs, Cyrille Regis and Dave Bennett. For City it was just the sort of start they wanted as they hoped for a good cup run. In difficult conditions – the pitch was hard and slippery after all the frost – the scene was right for a giant-killing act. The Sky Blues made sure that wouldn't happen with a positive, aggressive opening which left Bolton flattened as Downs and Regis scored in the 15th and 18th minutes. Bennett made sure by scoring his ninth of the season right on the stroke of half-time after a bad error from goalkeeper Mike Salmon. The majority of the players found the conditions difficult and tricky but they were made to measure for the Sky Blues' little midfield man Michael Gynn. He revelled in them and Bolton could never come to grips with his lightning-fast runs which always created panic and danger in their defence. City seemed content to coast their way to victory in the second half and the game lost most of its excitement or sparkle.

Neville Foulger was the *Coventry Evening Telegraph*'s chief football writer in 1987 and also the author of *Coventry City: The Complete History Of The Club* published in September 1979. His match reports could also be found in *The Pink*, the sports paper produced by the *Coventry Evening Telegraph* which would be delivered, 6pm on the dot, by a man in a van who drove around Coventry at breakneck speeds to throw bundles of the paper into newsagents' doorways to await fans eager to read how City had performed that day. *The Pink* was an institution and part of your matchday experience as was the 'Foulger Match File' where Neville rated the players out of ten for their matchday performance and gave a brief analysis of the game.

FOULGER MATCH FILE: 'It's a tribute to City's improvement this season that they were able to defuse so easily a potentially dangerous cup tie. Bolton were never given a chance to explode so the game didn't take off in terms of excitement or entertainment. In the FA Cup, though, only the result matters.'

NEVILLE FOULGER: When Coventry set out on the cup run on that freezing day at Highfield Road against Bolton I remember shivering up in the press box. When they beat them you thought, 'We're through,' but there was no reason to expect anything special with the draw to follow.

ANDY TURNER: I was part of the 'Class of '86' at Leeds University studying communication and cultural studies. The matches I could make were limited to the occasional trip back to the Midlands so the earlier rounds passed me by and were followed from afar until the quarter-final.

MICHAEL GYNN: George Curtis said to me, 'You're the first name on the team sheet today,' as the pitch was like a skating rink. They probably wouldn't have played the game in this day and age. It was really slippy and conditions suited my low centre of gravity.

George said after the game, 'You played really well today,' which was great to hear. It was my conditions, treacherous for everybody else, but great for me. It suited me and I'll always remember the tie.

GREG DOWNS: The first goal in the cup run was mine, I hit it quite well although I think the keeper helped it in a bit. It was a worked free kick with fellow full-back Brian Borrows's neat back-heel on a pitch that resembled an ice rink.

TREVOR PEAKE: The fact that Greg scored – his first for the club – was quite unusual. In those days full-backs did get forward but didn't get many goalscoring opportunities. At that point, the third round, you've got no idea if you're going on a cup run. I was in my fourth season at the club, the previous three cup runs and the ones after saw disaster quite early on so just getting through was an achievement even though they were Third Division at the time. It looked a comfortable tie for us on paper but, because I'd been there the previous three seasons, I knew never to take anything for granted.

STEVE OGRIZOVIC: At the start of every cup run, certainly when I played, third-round day could be a bit of a banana skin. We'd had some bad weather at the time of Bolton's visit, we won it comfortably but Bolton were not an easy side to face. It's always good to get into a competition, you want to get through the first few rounds because, if you don't, you feel like you've failed. It was a game we expected to win and we did a professional job.

DEAN EMERSON: We played well. Bolton were in the Third Division and we were favourites to win. It was a comfortable victory for us.

CALVIN URQUHART: The club kindly gave my family tickets to watch the match from the Main Stand of which I remember the game being absolutely freezing, however, a 3-0 victory helps you to forget! At the time I was so grateful for being allowed the opportunity to run out with my team, never even contemplating to think this would be the start of a victorious campaign. I do still believe that, to this day, I was a lucky mascot!

IAN BOLTON: I started working in radio while I was a student at Warwick University. I'd seen this little advert on the student station noticeboard that said, 'Local radio station looking for someone to prepare and read the 10:30pm sports bulletin'. After years of trying to get into broadcasting, suddenly a door opened for me. I made a tape, sent it off to Stuart Linnell at Mercia Sound, and got the job! Having finished the course at Warwick in the summer of 1985, I decided to give radio a go, rather than return to my previous career in engineering. I spent the 1985/86 season reporting on Nuneaton Borough in the Gola League on a Saturday afternoon with Richard Tanner who worked for the *Coventry Evening Telegraph*. By the start of 1986/87 I was on a contract at Mercia and I remember Stuart saying he'd like me to cover Coventry City. I recall the opening game, a 1-0 defeat at West Ham. I spoke with Greg Downs afterwards, I doubt he remembers but he was always very approachable. The *Coventry Evening Telegraph* headline when the third round draw was made in early December read 'Bolton at home'. Someone in the office at Mercia pinned it up and, before I left, I took the headline and pinned it to my bedroom door. I did on-air score updates from the match, with an off-air commentary, and then two reports at full time. There was one on the final whistle and another more considered report later on the Bolton victory on a freezing cold day at Highfield Road.

JIM BROWN: Bolton were easily beaten with the help of a great free kick from Greg Downs, his first goal in a City shirt.

KEV MONKS: When the third round draw was made, City were not playing particularly well. The FA Cup may have lost its magic in recent years nowadays with the likes of Manchester United and Arsenal fielding weakened sides but back in 1987 it was still the competition to win and when it came around, Bolton Wanderers at home, it was an important game as all ties were at the time. City pretty much breezed through with a 3-0 win.

ROB SUMMERFIELD: A bitterly cold day, I was under the weather, yet City shone through the winter gloom, mainly memorable for Greg Downs's free kick. Three up by half-time, it was a comfortable if low-key start.

DEAN NELSON: Two signings had been brought in, David Phillips and Keith Houchen, and it seemed the fun element had been restored as the players seemed more relaxed and united. Gates were still only just getting into double figures but the football was pleasing on the eye with a better balance to the side. It was bitterly cold that day as I took my place on the Sky Blue Terrace with the pitch frozen in places. Greg Downs's indirect free kick helped to warm us up followed by goals from Regis and Bennett to take us into round four.

LEE CORDEN: It wasn't easy being a City fan in Exhall in 1986. My journey began as City took on Liverpool in the Littlewoods Cup on a Wednesday night in November. There was a kid in the year above at school who 'supported' Liverpool and gave me stick every time he saw me in my Cov shirt. Under George and John, City had started 1986/87 reasonably well and I decided to call this kid's bluff and offer him a bet that Coventry would beat the mighty Reds that evening. It was probably only for a quid but that, to a schoolboy, was enough to mean something was riding on it. I wasn't at the game but, by all accounts, City did okay and had a 0-0 draw to show for their efforts which wasn't bad against the team who had dominated English football from the late 1970s. I know for a fact this kid wasn't at the match either. When I say he 'supported' Liverpool, he basically wore the kit and took the proverbial out of anyone (there weren't many of us) who did the right thing and supported their home town club. We agreed the bet would carry over into the replay which City duly lost 3-1 as Jan Molby scored a hat-trick of penalties. From the angle I watched them from on TV they all looked dubious so I refused to pay up. My dad and I were at Highfield Road for the Bolton tie as Regis, Bennett and Downs scored.

MOZ BAKER: In 1987 I worked for the DHSS on the counter, a bit like the TV series *Bread* but without the comedy. I sat in the Main Stand at Highfield Road as I reported on games for the local service for the blind. We did a weekly update on all things Coventry-sport related and reported on home matchdays doing interviews afterwards. I'd be in the press box at the back of the stand for home games then for away games be on the terraces with everyone else. There was no real inkling that this was the start of something great, it was a routine third round win and we moved on to think, 'Who will we get in round four?'

MATT PARTRIDGE: I have lots of memories from 1987, some more cloudy than others after all these years! The abiding memory from the Bolton tie was the cold, the FA Cup Final ticket vouchers in the matchday programme and Greggy Downs scoring his first goal for the club and celebrating in front of the West Terrace.

ROB GURNEY: The first game I went to was Coventry against Spurs in late 1979. I chose City because they were my local team and I should get behind them and had a chance of watching them regularly. We then had a season ticket for a few years before I started work at Mercia Sound. I then stopped going as I was always doing other things at the radio station on a Saturday trying to make myself useful with non-league football and the like. In 1987 I was 18 years old and went to the Bolton game. I was covering Nuneaton in the Conference so it was rare to be free on a Saturday but the weather ensured Borough was postponed that day. For Manchester United, Stoke and Sheffield Wednesday I was covering Nuneaton matches at various places and followed via the commentary on the radio.

BLAKE WAUGH: In 1987 I was in the second year at Finham Park, along with the author, the only Cov fans in our class and my school books were covered in City posters from *Match* and *Shoot* magazines. I was in the West Terrace for the Bolton tie, an expected win but nothing to get too excited about.

BOB EALES: In 1987 I was in my 11th year of my 24 in the Royal Navy. At the time of the Bolton game I was at sea in the Iceland Faroes gap, a place I was to see a lot of during the cup run. The trouble when you are at sea is you only have the radio and at that time we could only get the results and the one game that was on the radio. There were no newspapers so there was no real knowledge of the game apart from the result. I was happy with beating Bolton and so convincingly but the usual thought for me was, 'Oh well at least we have got through one game in the cup,' as a pessimistic fan.

ANDY SCAYSBROOK: I've been watching City for the last 43 years. In 1983 I'd begun my photographic career and was looking to leave the company I was working for and break out on my own. I had always wanted to create the moment of my first ever game, a night fixture against Wolves, when I walked into the ground and saw the most incredible sight of my young life – the players were out warming up and the sight of the sky blue shirts against the lush green of the illuminated pitch struck me like a lightning bolt. I had never seen a photograph of the ground taken at night so I decided to approach the club and see if they would let me shoot a picture of Highfield Road at night from the floodlights. I wrote a letter to George Curtis and a week later I had a reply. My heart was beating as I picked up the letter which had a Coventry City Football Club stamp on it. How I had dreamed of this moment as a kid, of the letter reading 'Coventry City would like to offer you a position in our central midfield', but I was equally as excited just by the fact the club had written to me. It was from George and he invited me to Highfield Road to talk further about my ideas.

I knew I had to make a good impression and cannot remember being as nervous as I made my way up King Richard Street to the reception. I swear the light disappeared as his huge muscular frame appeared in the doorway bearing that huge smile he wears so well, 'Hello Andy, I'm George, come in.' I sat down, looked him square in the eye and blurted out some words which, to this day, I can't remember what they were. I showed him my portfolio and spoke about my desire to be a press photographer. He smiled and said, 'I think it's a great idea, let's get it done!' George made me feel so welcome and said, 'I tell you what Andy, I will get this sorted for you and, if you like, you can have a press pass and cover some matches for us, we give you the pass, you give us some pictures for the matchday programme which will help you get some work for the newspapers. What do you think?' I couldn't believe the words he was saying, the smile on my face could have lit up Coventry for a year! I shook his hand and thanked him from the bottom of my heart for his time and generosity. He smiled and said, 'It's a pleasure, I look forward to seeing your work.'

I started shooting for the programme, the first time I saw my picture on the front cover was a moment I will never forget. You want to see your work used well and the buzz you get from a front page exclusive or a really good spread in a magazine never really leaves you. I've been fortunate to have my work published worldwide as well as in every UK newspaper but I can honestly say the biggest buzz I ever got from seeing my work in print was that programme cover as it was the start of a 30-year career as a press photographer. The picture was of Micky Adams and it appeared in the 1984 season against West Ham at Highfield Road.

By the beginning of the 1987 season I was getting regular covers and had become well known around the club on matchdays. I was friends with a number of players who treated me so well, there was none of this prima donna rubbish about these days. I had a great relationship with Cyrille, Benno, Killer, Lloydie and Peakey who was a great bloke always happy to help out. I would shoot the home games and also travel away mainly to shoot for my portfolio and other newspapers. I remember well the third round game at home to Bolton as I got a great shot of Greg Downs's goal. It was a straightforward win and I was delighted to get such a great shot from it.

ITV's *The Big Match* showed highlights that evening of Manchester United's 1-0 win over Manchester City, Arsenal's 3-1 victory at Reading and Caernarfon Town's goalless draw at home to Barnsley. Due to the freezing conditions the final tie of the round to be completed took place three weeks later on fourth round day as West Ham beat Orient 4-1. The highlight of round three saw Luton victorious against holders Liverpool after a second replay, albeit on the artificial pitch at Kenilworth Road while Tottenham defeated Scunthorpe United 3-2 at White Hart Lane.

Coventry Evening Telegraph, Monday 12 January 1987:

Britain in grip of Russia's icy blast

Britain today shivered in the grip of bitterly cold weather carried by winds from northern Europe and Russia. Many areas were experiencing their coldest day for years. Yesterday was the coldest in Coventry for 21 years and by mid-morning today the temperature in the city had reached only -7.5C.

It's United away
Tough but good chance says Peake

Unlucky Coventry City must travel to Old Trafford in the fourth round of the FA Cup. They have been paired against back-to-form Manchester United on 31 January – for the second time in three seasons. Central defender Trevor Peake was confident that they could still win through, 'Obviously we would have preferred a home match and this one at Highfield Road would have been a cracker. But we have no reason to fear taking on United at Old Trafford. There are worse places to go and I believe we have a great chance the way we are playing this season. It will be a difficult tie for us because United have started to improve a lot under Alex Ferguson's management. We'll come under a lot of pressure but if we can get through this one then we could go a long way in the competition.'

After the draw had been made City prepared for their first live television appearance as they travelled to leaders Arsenal for a 2.35pm kick-off at Highbury – on a Sunday. It was the first time Highbury had hosted live football as *The Big Match* came to north London.

The fixture was one of only ten to beat the adverse weather conditions due to Arsenal's £100,000 investment in their undersoil heating. The Pools Panel were in place and ready to make their call on the cancelled fixtures as only three First Division games went ahead that weekend with the investment in their respective pitch heating systems ensuring the fixtures at Everton and Manchester City took place. With Arsenal top of the First Division their stadium was half-full as only 17,561 watched City defend stoically for a point as neither side's defences could be breached.

This was followed by a disappointing 3-1 home defeat to West Ham as Tony Cottee plundered a hat-trick at Highfield Road. Prior to the tie at Old Trafford, Micky Adams signed for Second Division side Leeds United in a £110,000 deal on a two-and-a-half-year contract.

Coventry City Matchday Programme, Saturday 24 January 1987:

FA CUP TICKETS

Tickets for next Saturday's FA Cup fourth round tie against Manchester United at Old Trafford are now on sale at King Richard Street Ticket Office. They are priced: Seats £4.30, Terrace £2.80.

If a replay is necessary it will be at Highfield Road on Tuesday 3 February, kick-off 7.30pm. It will be ALL TICKET.

The Pink, Saturday 24 January 1987:

No need to fear them

'Who knows what's possible'

Tenacious Dean Emerson is convinced that City can crush the FA Cup hopes of the club he idolised as a boy. The former Stretford Ender returns to Old Trafford for the second time this season insisting that reviving United hold no fears, 'Only the brilliance of Chris Turner saved them from a beating back in November. If we play that well again and show half the spirit we had at Arsenal last Sunday then a good result is on the cards. Things are ticking over so well and our confidence is so high that there is no reason for us to fear anyone – home or away. Of course it's a tough tie but we can come through it. If we do, who knows what's possible given a little bit of luck.'

Take a gamble on us

Chief coach John Sillett had a spot of advice for those Sky Blues fans who liked a gamble. With City facing a demanding fourth round clash away to Manchester United, confident Sillett boldly declared, 'The time to back us is now. If we get through against United our odds will come tumbling down.'

At the moment Coral will offer you 50/1 and William Hill 40/1 against the Sky Blues winning the cup. One man, Sky Blues vice-chairman Ted Stocker, had placed £1,000 on City to lift the trophy back in September, at 50/1.

Nine-goal Dave Bennett lost his battle to return to City's line-up at Old Trafford with his troublesome thigh strain but Nick Pickering returned in place of Michael Gynn who joined Steve Sedgley on the substitutes' bench. Former Sky Blue Terry Gibson lined up for Alex Ferguson's side.

City: Steve Ogrizovic; Brian Borrows, Brian Kilcline, Trevor Peake, Greg Downs; David Phillips, Lloyd McGrath, Dean Emerson, Nick Pickering; Cyrille Regis, Keith Houchen. Subs: Michael Gynn, Steve Sedgley.

United: Chris Turner; John Sivebaek, Billy Garton, Kevin Moran, Mike Duxbury; Gordon Strachan, Norman Whiteside, Clayton Blackmore, Jesper Olsen; Frank Stapleton, Terry Gibson. Subs: Peter Davenport, Paul McGrath.

Referee: Ray Lewis (Great Bookham, Surrey).

Coventry Evening Telegraph, Monday 2 February 1987:

United they fall

Manchester United 0 Coventry City 1 (Houchen 20) Att: 49,082

Suddenly the fabled Twin Towers had become a magnetic attraction for the born-again Sky Blues. If anyone doubted their ability to go all the way, then this memorable triumph at Old Trafford – a soccer shrine if ever there was one – whipped up a tidal wave of optimism around the city. City's magnificent defence was the cornerstone of the victory clinched by a 20th-minute goal from Keith Houchen. Persistent and determined, he finally forced the ball home from close range at the third or fourth attempt.

FOULGER'S MATCH FILE: 'Severe frost and the failure of the Old Trafford undersoil heating system created a pitch on which only the brave prospered. City were braver and more determined than United. That was entertainment enough for the joyful Sky Blues fans in the big crowd. They have a team of which they can be proud.'

NEVILLE FOULGER: Most of us thought that was the end of the cup run when the draw was made but, they won 1-0, and that, in a sense, remains one of the great results. To win at Old Trafford it was almost then when you began to think, 'Is this going to be Coventry's year?'

STEVE OGRIZOVIC: United weren't then what they've been over the last generation but it's still formidable when you go to Old Trafford, back then they were a really big club and Alex Ferguson had just taken over. It was a great performance and a great victory as 'Roy of the Rovers' really stamped his mark on the competition with the winning goal. I don't think we realised at the time just what was going to happen but there was a definite feel after the United game, beating them away, and people started to think maybe it could be our year.

TERRY GIBSON: It was a cold day at Old Trafford, the pitch was half-frozen, covered by the stand, and this made footwear selection impossible. There were two moments that stood out in the game for me, my disallowed goal when Jesper Olsen pulled the ball back – it was out of play – and then in the second half I was through on goal and Trevor Peake brought me down. I tried to get into the penalty area but he was clever enough to prevent that but it would definitely have been a red in the modern era.

A couple of weeks prior to the Coventry tie I'd come on as substitute in the third round against Manchester City, a big game, local derby, then the week before I scored what turned out to be my only goal for United as we beat Arsenal 2-0. I was getting a chance under Alex Ferguson's management, I scored and made one and I was hopeful of a start against my old club. That was my main priority, I wasn't looking long-term, it was week-by-week, getting a game. I would have played against anybody just to have been playing regular football again.

Every team that wins the cup needs a result like the Manchester United win for Coventry to give total belief you can win it. Teams year after year believe their name is on the cup but you do need that win. I had it with Wimbledon the season after when we won at Newcastle in the fifth round, from then on we thought, 'We can win this.' That day for Coventry was clearly *the* day, it was a terrible draw for them to go to Old Trafford whatever state Manchester United were in at that time. In January 1985's fourth round clash I'd scored for Coventry in our 2-1 defeat at United and missed a penalty which was saved by Stephen Pears. Back then it wasn't a rarity to play on a frozen pitch. Prior to the United tie in 1985 we played in the snow against Manchester City at Highfield Road in round three. I scored twice with the orange tango ball and was desperate for a hat-trick so I could keep the unique ball!

There was no hairdryer at full time, United played well that day and it was one of those days where we just couldn't score a goal. The conditions weren't great but we plugged away, worked hard and came up against a team that defended brilliantly. They got their goal, got their noses in front, defended as a team, we couldn't break them down and they deserved their win. Coventry had total belief and didn't give us many opportunities to score. I don't think Alex would have had too many complaints, at that time we were on the up, he'd taken over and there were signs of improvement. The week before against Arsenal was a massive win for United as the Gunners had gone over 20 games unbeaten and it was his first game up against George Graham and Arsenal who were one of the top teams at the time. I was probably disappointed more than most as I'd just lost to my former club and at a club where I believed we might have a chance of winning something. I can't remember us creating too many chances even though we had plenty of the ball and Oggy was in inspired form on the day.

After the game I went home and watched it on *Match of the Day*. My main concern at that time was my own career, I didn't feel particularly gutted I'd lost to a former team and team-mates, I was just hoping for a career at Old Trafford with a new manager in place. For United it was the end of the season, that's why expectation was so high for us, we were off the pace in the league as when Fergie took over we were in the relegation zone.

As soon as we were knocked out it was the end of a lot of players' careers at United, it was a free-for-all in terms of speculation as back then you didn't have to wait until the end of the season to sign players. New players could come in at any time and it wasn't the easiest situation to deal with. If we had stayed in the cup a bit longer I might have hung around and played a few more games but it wasn't to be and I moved to Wimbledon in the summer of 1987, signed once again by Bobby Gould.

As an aside, while talking with Terry I had to ask him about his hat-trick for City in the 4-0 win over Liverpool in December 1983 at Highfield Road. I asked him what was going through his mind when, 3-0 up, he raced through on goal with only Bruce Grobbelaar to beat.

'I was thinking do I go for goal or pass to Gynny who had run about 70 yards. I was greedy and went for goal, I clipped it and while it's travelling past him and curling, I'm right behind it. It seemed like an age until it luckily hit the post and went in. We went in at half-time 3-0 up and thought they were still going to beat us 4-3, it was an unbelievable day. I've still got the ball, it got passed around the Liverpool players, only four of them signed it and was then booted out into the corridor that led to the pitch by Graeme Souness.'

GREG DOWNS: When you get drawn against them in the fourth round with Whiteside and company you think, 'Here we go, put the suits back on the hangers,' but we've gone up there and the state of the pitch worked in our favour. They were a good side in those days and on the day itself the pitch was quite frozen. 1986/87 was a bad winter and if you can recall the state of Highfield Road that year it was atrocious. Norman Whiteside played in boots where he had taken out the screw-in studs, the pitch was rock hard on a sunny day but it was freezing cold. We liked to play a bit ourselves and this helped us because it stopped United getting in behind us on the turn. George and John told us to play in front of ourselves, don't try and turn, play the way you're facing and we did. We got the breakthrough with a scrappy goal, I got down to the corner flag and I'm just trying to get it into the box, it wasn't the greatest cross but it got through to Houchen who prodded it home.

NICK PICKERING: I wore my astroturf trainers with the little pimples in the first half. Half of the pitch was frozen, then in the second half I wore my mouldies. It was a difficult game but we came through. The game was big because we knew we were playing good football and finished tenth at the season's end with a small squad. I thought after this game we had a great chance to win the cup. We had very under-rated players, David Phillips, Lloyd McGrath, every single one of them. Brian Borrows was a fantastic player, Trevor Peake I can't speak highly enough of, Killer, Oggy should have played for England, they all deserve a fantastic mention. Dave Bennett should have played for England, Cyrille more often.

TREVOR PEAKE: United were not the force they would become and we finished above them in the league (by seven points and a place). At the time we didn't realise the potential we had and our league position was considerably better than it had been before. Every season since I joined in the summer of 1983 we were fighting for our lives come May, and, because I'd witnessed the previous seasons when the draw was made it was a difficult tie, I suppose a lot of people were thinking, 'This could be the end for this year.' The game wouldn't have taken place nowadays, having said that, the pitches are now a lot better, there was a lot of frozen grounds at that time and we obviously benefitted on the day. It was difficult conditions but we managed to keep another clean sheet. While it was a really good result for us I didn't start thinking, 'This is our year.'

BRIAN BORROWS: What helped on the day was the frosty conditions. The pitch was hard and it was a leveller, not the main reason but a contributing factor. Once you start beating teams like that you start to think more optimistically and our league form was good too, it wasn't a fluke. The further you go, you start to think, 'This could be our year,' and it all just snowballed. Excitement grew in the city and the fans turned out in their numbers as they tended to do for the cup ties.

DEAN EMERSON: Sill used to take the lads away before each cup game and when we knew we had Manchester United in the next round we went off to Spain again. I looked forward to the game being a Manchester lad, all of my family were United supporters, I went from an early age until I began playing professionally. The conditions were tricky but we played ever so well to come away with the win.

KEITH HOUCHEN: You saw a lot of pitches in the 80s like that, you always played and they were rarely called off. You always used to lose the grass and because of the way stadiums were built you'd get half-thawed, half-frozen, as we did that day. United didn't have the greatest pitch. It was just a perseverance goal, I had about three or four attempts at it before I stabbed it over the line after battling Norman Whiteside. We played very well that day and had some cracking chances, we really could have won two- or three-nil. That sticks in my mind.

STUART LINNELL: I was managing director and programme controller of Mercia Sound throughout the cup run. The players were celebrating with the supporters at the final whistle and they didn't want the players to go. That was the moment I thought, 'If we can win here against this lot, just maybe...'

IAN WOODS: At the start of 1987 I was a news reporter at Mercia Sound. I'd switched from being the station's sports reporter the previous year and Ian Bolton had taken over as our football reporter. The fourth-round trip to Old Trafford wasn't to be missed so I went as a fan along with my mate Neil White. It was a cold day so I wore a sweater

I'd been given for Christmas, a bright canary yellow one. Naturally it became a lucky omen and I then had to wear it at every other match that season, even when it was far too warm as the cup run extended to springtime. I vividly remember Keith Houchen's goal that day because we were right behind the goal and saw his several attempts to bundle the ball into the net. Of course we were all thrilled and excited but I don't recall us thinking about winning the cup, it was still too early in the competition.

NEIL WHITE: Towards the end of 1986 I made two prophetic statements. Firstly, I said I would only get married if Coventry City won the FA Cup and when Ian Woods, Rob Gurney and I watched England play Northern Ireland at Wembley, I vowed I would only watch a cup final if City were in it. At the beginning of the cup run I was the sports editor of the *Sutton Coldfield News* which meant that I was watching a local team, Paget Rangers, instead of being at the third-round win against Bolton. I can't remember how I wriggled out of work but wild horses wouldn't have kept me away from Old Trafford in round four. I was joined by two good mates, Ian Woods and Steve Dimmock. Woodsie, who I had known from our days covering sport at Mercia Sound, was from Northern Ireland but had become an honorary Sky Blue fan and Steve was a West Brom supporter who thought it would be a good game. All I can remember from the match was that the ball seemed to ping around the penalty area for an age before Keith Houchen's shot went in.

KEV MONKS: I've always enjoyed a trip to Manchester United. Before the invasion of the day trippers and United having a global following thanks to the television explosion of the early 1990s, Old Trafford was always a good place for a drink and day out. It was also the scene of City defeats down the years but the FA Cup fourth round draw was not to be a day when we left heading off to drown our sorrows. I was telling my mates in the pub before the game that City would lose. Being a gambler with little to no luck I had opted for a bit of reverse psychology in the hope that by saying Coventry City would not win, they actually would. The game progressed well, I was stood on the terrace in the away end surrounded by friends and we held our breath as Keith Houchen had a shot. I shouted out, 'Hit the thing!' as he took another kick at the ball and, after what seemed an absolute age, the ball trickled over the line and into the net. Celebrations of any City goal at the time were mental and we went ballistic at what proved to be the only goal of the game. The fourth round saw some of the favourites going out of the competition and there was talk in the pubs, especially the Rose and Crown on the Walsgrave Road where I used to drink, that City were in with a good chance of a cup run.

MATT PARTRIDGE: The proper FA Cup started at Old Trafford in round four. We made our way up there on the coach with no expectation at all. Playing against former fans' favourite 'Gibbo' [Terry Gibson] plus many other internationals, I recall the ball being crossed by Greg Downs and bouncing off all parts of Houchen's anatomy before landing in the net. The joy was unimaginable and has been saved to history by the fact that I am caught on camera by *Match of the Day* behind the goal, head through the fences, giving it loads to coin a phrase!

MATT KERR: I went to every round but, prior to the trip to Manchester, I'd sprained my ankle and wasn't going to go as I could hardly walk. For each cup tie I was with my Grandad Arthur and my cousin, when Keith Houchen scored I jumped up and fell over such was the pain. When we came out of Old Trafford I was in agony and my cousin flagged down a police van to help me and give us a lift to where our coach was parked. They opened the van doors and asked if I was United or Coventry. When we replied they shut the doors and drove off! My cousin was livid but then a patrol car came past and stopped to help. The next day I went back to hospital and they told me I had fractured my ankle in two places.

BLAKE WAUGH: We caught the British Rail special. I was with my brother, Jason, and his mates; me a 12-year-old on his first ever visit to Old Trafford. The game was a scrappy affair and Keith Houchen scored arguably the ugliest goal I've ever seen.

ROB SUMMERFIELD: After the Bolton win three of us congregated in work's rest room for the draw, live on the radio at 12.30pm. 'Man Utd away!' 'Well, it's a day out,' said one lad with our typical but this time misguided pessimism. I turned up at Coventry railway station fully clad in black. It was my goth phase. 'It's Johnny Cash! He's come as the ref!' yelled my comedian friends. My main memory is how this was no day out but witnessing eleven men on a mission. The belief transferred to the fans with a neat Houchen finish and Oggy's safe hands. That night, I uttered for the first time 'We will win this.' It wasn't the bravado of an Old Trafford win but sensing something in the air, courtesy of a man called Sillett.

LEE CORDEN: If truth be told, if we had drawn Stoke City in the fourth round, my brag of being at every match would probably never have come true because it was only the fact that City were drawn to play at Old Trafford in the next round that spurred my dad on to take us to an away game. We'll all look back now and say we knew our name was on the cup but I think most City fans thought this was their 'cup final' even though United were far less of a force than they went on to become in the 1990s. I hadn't been to many away games then and I do remember how special it felt getting the matchday programme and looking around the stadium with terraces at the sides as well as at the ends of the ground. I remember the feeling when Houchen forced the ball over the line for probably the scrappiest goal of the cup run to take us through. We sat in the car after the game as the other results came through on the radio and I started to plot a path through to the final. 'If we get x at home in the next round and then y in the quarter-final that would give us a great chance of getting to the semi-final and then, who knows?' My dad and brother quickly scoffed that I was getting ahead of myself.

MOZ BAKER: It was the first time I'd ever been to Old Trafford. The FA Cup back then was the big thing, there was something really exciting about going to a big stadium and I was in the terrace behind the goal in among a very vocal support that day. In the lead-up to the game, with my work for the blind, we contacted Alex Ferguson, who hadn't long been in charge, and he gave us so much of his time to talk about the game. Given the amount of media who want to speak to him prior to and after a game I always respected him for that. Even though it wasn't the best

United side it still wasn't a game we perhaps expected to win so to go there and win was some effort.

DEAN NELSON: It was up to Old Trafford and Alex Ferguson's Manchester United, he had only been in charge since November and was still trying to get his thoughts across to his players. Keith Houchen scored as the ball seemed to rebound off him half a dozen times and United's right-back John Sivebaek was unable to clear it off the line. We took a good following that day and they were booed off at the final whistle.

ANDY SCAYSBROOK: The draw was made and we got United away, any other season we would have thought, 'Oh well, maybe next year,' but not this time. The belief was strong with the fans, our season was going very well and we would be up against our old West End hero, Terry Gibson. Hessie, John, Andy and myself had decided we were good luck charms and should travel together for the rest of the competition. So on that freezing January morning we set off for Manchester. Optimism was in the air and we laughed our heads off exchanging banter and more than a few beers on our way to Old Trafford. The support that day sent tingles down my spine, we sang the roof off Old Trafford and put the Mancs to shame. We were stood right behind the goal where Houch scored, I can remember him stretching out that leg to prod the ball home and the City fans went ballistic. I found myself on the floor among a mass of seething, laughing bodies as we celebrated, everybody helping each other up and hugging each other in celebration – I get goosebumps just thinking about that – this was the reason we were fans, to celebrate such achievement against all the odds, it's something non-football fans will never understand.

BOB EALES: I thought, 'We'll never beat them, not at Old Trafford, the run will be over at the second hurdle.' With so many people on a ship there is an awful lot of banter between everyone and I was keeping my head down from the United fans. I was generally the only Sky Blues fan on most ships, to my amazement when the results came in we had won 1-0 and that head of mine came straight above the parapet sniping at the Red Devils supporters.

The Sky Blues' victory at Old Trafford was featured on the BBC's *Match of the Day* along with Wimbledon v Portsmouth and Bradford v Everton. Central TV would show Watford v Chelsea live the following day.

Highlights of round four saw Third Division Wigan Athletic beat Norwich 1-0 at Springfield Park, with the Canaries then sixth in the First Division, while leaders Everton won 1-0 at Bradford City. Tottenham triumphed 4-0 against Crystal Palace while Stoke City continued their fine run in Division Two with a 2-1 victory against Cardiff City.

On the same day City triumphed at Old Trafford, Mick Coop's youth team travelled to The Dell to face Southampton in the FA Youth Cup third round. A superb defensive performance saw the side frustrate a strongly fancied Saints team who had scored over 100 goals in the season. The 13 on duty down on the South Coast comprised Paul Bastock, Howard Clark, Tony Dobson,

John Gowens, Anthony Smith, Robert Smith, Michael Cook, Paul Jones, Gary Marshall, Steve Livingstone, Paul Shepstone, Mark Pollard and Chris Galley.

The Southampton side included Alan Shearer, Matt Le Tissier, Tommy Widdrington, Francis Benali, Neil Maddison, Keith Grainger, Allen Tankard and Rod and Ray Wallace.

Coventry Evening Telegraph, Monday 2 February 1987:

It's Stoke away!

Coventry City were today drawn away to Stoke City in the fifth round of the FA Cup on 21 February. It means that the Sky Blues will be breaking new ground in the competition – it is their first meeting with Stoke in the FA Cup. After the magnificent win over Manchester United at Old Trafford last Saturday the Sky Blues had hoped for a home draw in the fifth round. But they will still fancy their chances of progressing to the quarter-finals at the Victoria Ground.

The draw

Leeds v QPR
Tottenham v Newcastle United
Walsall v Watford
Sheffield Wednesday v West Ham
Stoke City v COVENTRY CITY
Wimbledon v Everton
Wigan Athletic v Hull City
Arsenal v Barnsley

After the euphoria of their triumph at Old Trafford in front of over 49,000 fans City came down to earth with a bump as Glenn Cockerill's brace took the points for Southampton at The Dell, their side including Peter Shilton, Mark Dennis, Jimmy Case, Mark Wright and David Armstrong. Dean Emerson's yellow card took him over the disciplinary points limit and he would miss the FA Cup trip to Stoke City as a result.

Four days later the trip to Goodison Park, Everton, returned the same result. Gary Stevens, Trevor Steven and Adrian Heath overturned Cyrille Regis's early strike to move City down to tenth as the eventual champions galvanised 30,000 supporters to take the points.

A further blow saw Lloyd McGrath's yellow card also rule him out of the Stoke tie as he too crossed the disciplinary points threshold. This left John Sillett and George Curtis with a selection headache with both McGrath and Emerson absent for the trip to the Potteries.

Mick Coop's youth team triumphed 3-2 in their Youth Cup third round replay with Southampton. Goals from Steve Livingstone, Paul Jones and a Michael Cook penalty took them on to a clash with Oldham Athletic at Boundary Park on their artificial pitch.

A timely lift, after three league defeats in succession, saw Highfield Road raise the roof after Lloyd McGrath's first goal for the club in the 3-0 defeat of Chelsea. McGrath's left-footed strike flew into Tony Godden's net as half-time approached and, both his celebration, along with the crowd's were on a par with when Brian 'Harry'

Roberts opened his account in December 1982 at West Ham after 192 first-team games.

Brian Kilcline's penalty, smashed home in his usual trademark style, and Nick Pickering completed the scoring as confidence soared ahead of the trip to Stoke.

LLOYD McGRATH: I'd been in the team for three/four seasons and never scored. Greg Downs played it in, it was headed back down to me and I've hit it left-footed into the top corner. It was a great moment for me to finally score after all that time.

Coventry City Matchday Programme, Saturday 14 February 1987: FA CUP TICKETS

Tickets for next Saturday's FA Cup fifth round tie against Stoke City at the Victoria Ground are now on sale at King Richard Street Ticket Office. They are priced: Seats £6. Terrace £3. There are no reduction for senior citizens and juveniles.

It is an ALL TICKET match and therefore you must purchase tickets in advance. They will be on sale at King Richard Street Ticket Office until 4pm on Friday 20 February, subject to availability.

If a replay is necessary it will be at Highfield Road on Tuesday 24 February, kick-off 7.30pm. It will be an ALL TICKET match.

Coventry Evening Telegraph, Saturday 14 February 1987:

Phillips out of Welsh game

Coventry City have pulled Dave Phillips out of the Welsh squad to face Russia in Cardiff on Wednesday. They don't want to risk the midfield man being injured for next Saturday's vital FA Cup fifth round clash at Stoke City. City boss George Curtis said today, 'With Dean Emerson and Lloyd McGrath suspended and Martin Lane cup-tied we are down to the bare bones for the Stoke match. We will have only 12 senior professionals from which to choose our side and we have to put the interests of the club and our supporters first. Had the Welsh match been a competitive one then we would have put their interests first and allowed Phillips to play. But as it is only a friendly we have asked them to release him. It's the only thing we could have done in the circumstances.'

Coventry Evening Telegraph, Friday 20 February 1987:

Excitement at fever pitch on eve of cup clash

We dare not lose – Oggy

Goalkeeper Steve Ogrizovic today labelled Coventry City's fifth round FA Cup tie as 'The game we daren't lose'. And with excitement at fever-pitch on the eve of City's trip to Second Division Stoke, optimistic Oggy predicted, 'We can do it – but it will be a hell of a match.' He was backed by striker Keith Houchen, the Sky Blues match-winning hero in the fourth round at Old Trafford, 'It is going to be a hard game – but it shouldn't be any harder than Manchester United. If we put our game together we can win.'

Victory would put City into the quarter-finals for the first time since 1982 and for only the fifth time in their history. An army of 8,000 Sky Blues fans in the packed Victoria Ground will be willing them to do it.

The pitch was expected to be rock hard with overnight frost forecast. John Sillett and George Curtis selected Michael Gynn in midfield at the expense of Steve Sedgley who shared bench duties with Graham Rodger. Gynn and the fit-again Dave Bennett replaced suspended Lloyd McGrath and Dean Emerson with Bennett joined in central midfield by David Phillips as Gynn lined up on the right of midfield.

City supporters were given the complete Stoke End Stand as, in addition to the many coaches and cars, two special trains were commissioned by British Rail to take the Sky Blues hordes to Stoke.

Stoke City Matchday Programme, Saturday 21 February 1987:

MICK MILLS (Stoke player-manager): 'I would like to offer a very warm welcome to Coventry City. I have been very impressed with Coventry over the years, on how they have been able to make the most from all activities concerning a football club, although from the playing side they haven't had all that much success.

Yet it must not be forgotten the length of time they have stayed in the First Division and the progress made this year, it is their promotional ability and commercial activities that are as good as anywhere.

The game today looks very nicely balanced between two teams enjoying good seasons. The response from the public again needs some mentioning and we very much appreciate your support and hope that you see a cracking game.'

City: Steve Ogrizovic; Brian Borrows, Brian Kilcline, Trevor Peake, Greg Downs; Michael Gynn, Dave Bennett, David Phillips, Nick Pickering; Cyrille Regis, Keith Houchen. Subs: Steve Sedgley, Graham Rodger.

Stoke: Peter Fox; Lee Dixon, Steve Bould, George Berry, Steve Parkin; Tony Ford, Tony Kelly, Brian Talbot, Phil Heath; Nicky Morgan, Carl Saunders. Subs: Keith Bertschin, Chris Hemming.

Referee: Robert Nixon (Merseyside).

Coventry Evening Telegraph, Monday 23 February 1987:

Wembley dream is still on

Stoke City 0 Coventry City 1 (Gynn 71) Att: 31,255

Polished and purposeful Coventry City are on the edge of greatness. One more FA Cup win will create club history – two will realise a glorious dream. They have never progressed beyond the last eight – but don't back against them doing it this time. The Sky Blue song promises to become a real tune of glory. City's army of 8,000 fans belted it out in delight at the Victoria Ground as Michael Gynn finally fired in the all-important goal in the 71st minute. It was enough to settle a titanic tie, packed with drama and liberally laced with incident and excitement.

At the end of it all Stoke claimed they should have had a penalty and insisted the decisive goal was offside.

FOULGER MATCH FILE: 'Not a classic in terms of pure football but an absolute cracker of a cup-tie. Stoke did themselves proud and possibly deserved a replay. The Sky Blues didn't play as well as they can – but their heads never dropped and their spirit never wilted.'

NEVILLE FOULGER: It wasn't the greatest of games but City battled through and suddenly they were in the quarter-finals. Was it a penalty? You look back, they've won it 1-0, with those sort of things happening you start to think was lady luck on their side and any side that goes on to win the FA Cup has that fortune at some stage. At Stoke, some referees would have given it, others not, but it was an argument. That again was a moment, 'Is this going to be our year?'

JOHN SILLETT: That was a hard game at Stoke. We had a young apprentice then, Steve Cockrill, he was a lad who trained so hard to get in the youth team and was then struck down with injury. I called him in on the Friday and said, 'You're coming with me, you're coming in the dressing room to do the boots and any odd jobs we need doing.' I called him our lucky mascot and told him, 'Never mind about playing for the youth team, you're coming with us.' He was so happy and we took him on the bus to every game. Steve was brilliant in the dressing room – players are very precise before a match with their kit, everything has to be right, I wanted everything right and he got it right.

Was it a penalty? I must admit I held my breath, I honestly thought at the time that it was, you always think every decision is going to go against you because you can't influence anything from the dugout. I took a deep breath and said to physio George Dalton, 'We've got away with it there.'

GEORGE DALTON: We decided to take an apprentice to help with the kit and Steve was on duty. John said to him that as long as we were still in the cup we'd keep him and he went everywhere with us.

DAVID PHILLIPS: I believe I gave a penalty away and the referee never gave it. At the time I did think it was a foul for my tackle on Lee Dixon, I just looked at the referee who waved play on. My heart, which had sank to my bowels, rose up and I was so delighted he never gave it. For the goal I looked at the better option when Nick Pickering's cross reached me in the Stoke area. It wasn't sitting right so to move the ball out to Micky proved the correct decision in the end. A really difficult game, we weren't at our best but we saw it through.

LEE DIXON: I really can't remember the game! Just the penalty shout, I don't even know who tripped me. Was it a penalty? Absolutely, 100 per cent.

MICHAEL GYNN: It was something I did in my early days at Peterborough – when the ball came to me I passed it into the net, if you've got good technique and a short back lift like I had you pick your spot and I just thought, 'This is going in the corner.' You don't think about it, you weigh up the situation and within a split second you've done it. If I'd taken a touch Steve Parkin would have closed me down but I hit it first time and didn't give Peter Fox time to think – it was past him before he could move. It was a heavy pitch that day with a few bobbles going around and it was another important goal I scored in front of the City supporters. It was a tough game and a typical FA Cup match, we had a lot of resilience then and it was a fantastic result for us in front of 30,000-plus fans at a packed Victoria Ground.

CYRILLE REGIS: Was it a penalty? The referee didn't give it so it couldn't have been [chuckles] – it wasn't a classic, cup games are like that, you get through to the next round and face the next challenge.

KEITH HOUCHEN: In the whole cup run that was the day we got out of jail a little bit. Stoke were probably better than us on the day, we rode our luck quite a bit, again it wasn't a great pitch, very muddy and heavy. I remember them having a real shout for a penalty that I would have given. As a forward you're looking back at the play and that was one of them where I thought, 'Oh no.' The atmosphere was unbelievable, they really went at us for a while but we had this horrible habit of soaking up the pressure and nicking goals out of nothing which Micky Gynn did. In the cup run we deserved to win every match but they really tore at us and we rode our luck for quite a time.

BRIAN KILCLINE: We'd had to play at Stoke the year before in the relegation battle. In my mind there wasn't the pressure we'd had in the league game, it's just like a normal game of football because you don't think you're going to get to the final. It's another game and, to be fair, the inspiration was Sill taking us away for a trip before every cup round!

TREVOR PEAKE: I've got to say I did think it was a penalty – you glance to the referee and then a second later when you know the whistle's not gone, you're thankful it hasn't been given. Sometimes that might be the luck you need to go through but they were flying at the top of the Second Division, it was a really tricky fixture in the sense more than the Manchester United game, the reward was a quarter-final place. That may have been when I started to think it was our year, depending on the draw. It was a horrible pitch, they had Lee Dixon and Steve Bould, and were on an unbeaten run.

GREG DOWNS: I don't remember a great deal about the game. The pitch was a quagmire. I don't think it was a penalty, you get to that desperation stage where you just try to get something and Lee Dixon was as honest a player as you'll see. They had a full house, the first time in a long time and I believe on the day we were the more accomplished side. We kept the ball and had a good inner resolve among us. We had a team that could rise to situations and battle their way through and that stood us in good stead for the ties to come.

BRIAN BORROWS: It was a very difficult game, a tough tie and Stoke were certainly not an easy side to play as they were doing well in the Second Division.

NICK PICKERING: It was a massive, muddy pitch at the Victoria Ground. I was up and down the left against

Lee Dixon, he's the only full-back who caused me loads of trouble, he was bombing on and I was having to chase him on a muddy pitch. I got away from him in the last 25 minutes and managed to cross the ball for the winning goal.

GRAHAM RODGER: We had a good, experienced team and in those days it was harder for younger players to break into the side. I can recall practise matches in training and we had two teams that could rival each other. Those decisions [penalty] are ones that make history. Phillo's a great lad, if he said he believed it was a penalty, it probably was! He's an extremely honest person. I was young at the time [19] and perhaps a bit headstrong so when I look back on that period one of the biggest influences was the management team. John Sillett's man management was from another planet. He brought together a mismatch of players, a few journeymen, a few internationals and stuck them together to produce a really, really strong First Division team. I was disappointed I wasn't playing more but I had to go past Brian Kilcline and Trevor Peake who were an outstanding partnership, they complemented each other so well. You learned all the time as a young player. I remember Dave Bennett, in centre midfield that day, made a mistake and John Sillett got up and bawled at him but he'd already made his recovery run, he couldn't get back the ball he'd given away but when it came into the box he'd spotted the danger and was there to clear. You took note of this as a young player and learnt continually from these players.

STEVE OGRIZOVIC: Stoke City were a good side, they played well and there was a great atmosphere at the ground. Our fans really got behind us, we did very well to make what looked a tricky away tie into a win – we felt the weight of the support that day. It was a really good result and one of the trickiest ties – they had a number of players who went on to better things. After winning at Old Trafford we had to follow it up with a win at Stoke otherwise it would have been a real waste of the win in Manchester. There was plenty of motivation for us at Stoke that day.

STEVE SEDGLEY: I was 18 at the time and used to end up on the bench for the cup games, like a superstition almost. I was always eager to play, any chance I got to go on I just tried to do my best. I listened to the experienced players, they organise you, talk you through it and my enthusiasm carried me through. There was plenty of experience in that side and Stoke was a tough place to play. It was a fantastic result.

LLOYD McGRATH: I was in the stands watching as I was suspended and it was one of the hardest games in the cup run.

STEVE COCKRILL: I joined City in 1985 as an associate schoolboy, aged 15, when Don Mackay was manager. I used to come down from Hartlepool in the school holidays and was then offered an apprenticeship. We used to live in the club houses on Catherine Street just off the back of the West Stand at Highfield Road and would find our way into the Mercers Arms on a Wednesday night, Park Lane on a Saturday. I was with Michael Cook, Steve Livingstone and Steve Sedgley among others. I turned 17 in cup final year and was in my first year with the youth team. It all happened by chance as I injured my back, quite a bad injury, and at the time we couldn't work out what the problem was.

George Dalton tried to get me back on my feet but it was a freak injury and probably turned out to be the difference between being offered a professional contract. I came back from the injury and had lost a bit of pace. I was with the first team for the Bolton tie but didn't go to Manchester United because the youth team had an FA Youth Cup tie against Southampton at The Dell so I'd travelled with them that day. I couldn't play but we drew 0-0 and won the replay. They had Shearer, Le Tissier, Benali, Widdrington, Maddison and the Wallace brothers [Rod and Ray] in their squad. From Stoke onwards I was travelling with the first team pretty much all the time because I couldn't play. Stoke was a tough game, Lee Dixon and Steve Bould were in their team, they had a good side and gave us a bit of a mauling. I sat on the bench with the boss, it was fantastic, a surreal experience. I went with the team to league games too and, whenever I did go [on away trips], they didn't get beat. It was unbelievable. I was doing the kit and boots and helped out in the dressing room.

JOHN POYNTON: That was a definite penalty but that's luck for you. I've always said in the course of a season they generally level themselves out.

JIM BROWN: Coming out of Stoke's Victoria Ground on that February afternoon singing the Sky Blue song I just had the feeling that something special was brewing. Although they were a Second Division side Stoke had battered us only for Micky Gynn to snatch the only goal. The Sky Blue Army were convinced but the floating fans were still not impressed – a week later there were just 12,000 at Highfield Road to see us play Charlton. The win at Old Trafford, while a shock, wasn't the big thing it would be these days but it was this win at Stoke that made me realise this could be our year. Having been a City fan since the early 1960s, however, I knew that my team could easily let me down. In 1973 I thought we were a sure bet for Wembley but we blew it at Molineux. Then, a good League Cup run the following year raised expectations but home advantage over Manchester City in the quarter-final was wasted. In 1981 we got close to Wembley until West Ham's Jimmy Neighbour snatched the prize away in a League Cup semi-final second leg at Upton Park with over 36,000 present.

MOZ BAKER: I thought it was a penalty at the time. We were behind the goal again and the Victoria Ground pitch was muddy and a real leveller. I'd only been there once before back in 1985 when Stuart Pearce's penalty gave us a 1-0 win in the first of three games we needed to win to stay up. We did well to come through the tie, it was a tough game. After the United game the excitement had started to build, you had the cup draw at lunchtime on a Monday and it was all about the football, the draw would be made live on radio rather than on TV and you stopped what you were doing to hear the next round's opponents.

MATT PARTRIDGE: We went off to Stoke with a lot more confidence and this was probably the hardest game of the run up to Wembley. They battered us and had a lot of near misses. It was reported in the *ahem* Sunday Sport that Micky had scored with a header! On we marched!

MATT KERR: I was in plaster and on a crutch since the United tie and we were in the seats this time. I had a season ticket with my granddad Arthur between the ages of 13 and 15, and along with my cousin we stuck together as we won each game, a kind of superstition. We didn't want to break the run.

BLAKE WAUGH: Jimmy Greaves on Central Sport kept saying we couldn't win the cup but the city was starting to believe. We had a great spine to the team, all great players and terrific professionals. City were a match for anyone but Stoke was a potential banana skin and we were lucky to get through on the day.

KEV MONKS: Cup fever was beginning to take hold and the Sky Blues sold out their allocation of tickets. Not as packed, though, as it was in May 1985 when Stuart Pearce's penalty helped keep us in the top flight but full enough.

DANNY FINLAY: The only game I didn't go to was Stoke in round five. My dad always said that back in the 1980s there was still a bit of trouble around and I was 11 at the time. There was no way he was going to take me to the game and he always stood by the decision as, on the way to the game, a load of Stoke fans tried to run him and his pals off the road. They cut them up in their car, deliberately, when they saw the sky blue flags flying from the windows. His mate went up on to the gravel on the side of the road on the turn-off to Stoke from the M6.

ANDY SCAYSBROOK: I travelled with my friends to Stoke, Andy Perryman, John Reader and our old mate, Hessie. Gynny's goal made our day and we travelled back to Cov via a few pubs and talked about the impossible dream.

'You know what lads, I think we could get to Wembley this year,' said John. Any other year that would have been the talk of a madman but things were different this year, we were playing with a style that suited the team, we had a great outlet in 'Benno' on the wing and the players were scrapping it out, playing their hearts out for each other. It was the best team spirit I had ever seen from a Coventry side and we loved it. No big stars, no prima donnas, just good, solid players grafting it out for each other and the fans were loving it!

The City was starting to believe, the league was going well and 'Snoz' and George had the total respect of both fans and players. For the first time ever I was certain good things were going to happen, you just felt it in your bones. We had a passion about us that I hadn't seen before, a belief and sense of unity that was a pleasure to see and be a part of. The Sky Blue Army was in full voice everywhere we went around the country with pride in our team and huge vocal support. As all the cup games were away I didn't have to shoot any pictures which was a relief as I'm not sure how well I would have worked under such delirium.

ROB SUMMERFIELD: I always call this the best game I never saw. We got the last train from Cov station. The Victoria Ground away end was rammed, I always loved that ground, old school, but I only ever saw parts of the pitch at once that day. It was a typical cup tie and Stoke pushed us hard. They missed a headed sitter, were denied a good penalty shout but the Sky Blues dug in. Micky Gynn snapped up a half-chance and terrace mayhem ensued. That Coventry team could play but that was a grafters' victory. Just as the numbers of fans had steadily grown, the rest room at work was packed for the quarter-final draw. The magic of the cup had really arrived.

LEE CORDEN: Drawing Stoke away did, however, seem like a bye to the next round with the form City were in but our hopes of a comfortable win were dashed. It was another afternoon standing on a terrace down near the front and was decided by another solitary goal. I'd only been going to watch the Sky Blues for a couple of seasons but they now seemed invincible and I definitely took for granted that this is how it would always be.

DEAN NELSON: Stoke at the time were in the old Second Division and going well. The Sky Blue Army were out in force as they took over the away end with fans climbing the perimeter fence when Michael Gynn sent them into raptures as he put away the winner. Now fans were starting to dream of things to come and the next round couldn't come quick enough.

IAN WOODS: By the time the fifth round tie at Stoke came around, I'd been drafted back into the Mercia Sound sports team. I used to present *Sportacular* – the Saturday afternoon sports programme – and was asked to fill in as the studio presenter while Mike Liggins did the match commentary from the Victoria Ground. By the time the final whistle was blown we really could start dreaming of a visit to Wembley.

NEIL WHITE: Woodsie decided his yellow jumper was the lucky omen and Steve was so taken with the display at

Old Trafford that he agreed to come to Stoke. We stood behind the goal and the fans went ballistic as Micky Gynn drove in the winner.

BOB EALES: The Stoke game was another game that I did not expect us to win especially as we were away from home again but when the result came in I was delighted as you can imagine.

Highlights of round five saw Dave Bassett's 'Crazy Gang' defeat soon-to-be champions Everton 3-1 at Plough Lane live on *Match of the Day* while Sheffield Wednesday would overcome a replay at Upton Park to win 2-0 against West Ham. Third Division Wigan overcame Second Division Hull City 3-0 at Springfield Park while Tottenham's 1-0 win against Newcastle at White Hart Lane saw them into the hat for the last eight, as they went in search of their eighth FA Cup success.

Coventry Evening Telegraph, Monday 23 February 1987:

AWAY AGAIN!

Now Sky Blues must go to Wednesday or West Ham

Wembley hopefuls Coventry City will have to travel again in the quarter-finals of the FA Cup. They have been drawn to visit the winners of the fifth-round replay between West Ham and Sheffield Wednesday on 14 March. It's another demanding challenge for the Sky Blues, who had to win successive away ties at Manchester United and Stoke to reach the last eight. City are in the last eight for the first time since 1982 and for only the fifth time in their history. They have never reached the semi-finals. John Sillett today described City's exploits as a 'return to the 60s'. He added, 'I remember those days – thank God they are back.

'When George Curtis and myself went out on to the pitch at Stoke an hour before the kick-off the reception they gave us was incredible. I think they made me work even harder and better in terms of geeing up the lads before the kick-off. I just felt there was no way we could let them down. I kept our dressing room windows open so that the players could hear the fans sing the Sky Blue song – it was marvellous – the best I've heard it since the 60s.'

The draw
Arsenal v Watford
Wimbledon v Tottenham Hotspur
Sheffield Wednesday v COVENTRY CITY

Wigan Athletic v Leeds United
Matches to be played on 14 March

Mick Coop's youth team drew 0-0 with Oldham Athletic in their FA Youth Cup fourth round tie.

Coventry City Matchday Programme, Saturday 28 February 1987:

FA CUP TICKETS

The FA Cup quarter-final match against Sheffield Wednesday at Hillsborough on 14 March will be ALL TICKET.

PRICES
Seats £5.50 for adults, £3.50 juveniles and senior citizens.
Terraces £3.50 adults, £2.00 juveniles and senior citizens.

If a replay is necessary it will be at Highfield Road on Wednesday 18 March, kick-off 7.30pm.

As cup fever hit Coventry with a vengeance the league campaign continued with City eighth in the First Division. The visit of Charlton saw a 2-1 victory ground out against

Coventry Evening Telegraph, Tuesday 3 March 1987:

Sales of City's allocation of 14,000 tickets for the cup tie at Hillsborough began today to season ticket holders and Executive Club members. They will go on sale to the general public from Thursday and the Sky Blues hope to sell all 14,000. They have 10,000 for the terrace and 4,000 seats. British Rail will again be putting on a Sky Blue special for the occasion at a cost of £7 return. A total of 1,035 City fans travelled by rail to Stoke and British Rail reported a trouble-free day.

opposition fighting for their lives at the bottom of the table. Goals by Greg Downs and Cyrille Regis were sandwiched by an equaliser from former Sky Blue Jim Melrose who, back in 1982, hit a hat-trick on his home debut against Everton at Highfield Road.

With Sheffield Wednesday having knocked West Ham out of the cup with a fine performance in east London, City would face them twice in seven days with the league clash at Highfield Road prior to the cup clash. Lloyd McGrath's goal took the points on a quagmire of a pitch as the fixture took place in blizzard conditions.

The one huge negative for Sky Blues supporters saw influential Dean Emerson stretchered off with a knee injury after a clash with Gary Megson. At the time, no one realised just how serious the injury would be for the brilliant young midfielder. Only 30 games were played in the Football League that day – 7 March – as the freezing conditions continued to play havoc with the fixture list.

DEAN EMERSON: I injured my knee a week prior to the quarter-final. It was a clash of knees and happened early on in the first half. I carried on playing and it was only after I'd cooled down at half-time and then gone back out for the second half that it gave way when I put weight on it.

IAN BOLTON: The last game I reported on for Mercia Sound was the 1-0 league victory over Sheffield Wednesday a week prior to the quarter-final. It was a snowy day and Mike Liggins was presenting *Sportacular*. At the end of the programme, he mentioned on air it was my last game working for Mercia and said to me, 'What do you think about it being Coventry's year for the FA Cup?' I remember saying, 'Well, why not? My team [Chelsea] aren't in it any more, why not!' My contract expired at the end of March and I joined Radio WM in Birmingham to present just sport. At Mercia I was also a presenter on the Sunday *Night Express* (10pm–1am) and filled in on the other programmes. When the station went 24-hour I presented the early morning show (4am–7am) and I'd be up at 2.30am five days a week then covering Coventry on a Saturday wherever they were. I'd also been working for Coventry Cable. It was all very exciting and great to be around. I covered the victories over Bolton, Manchester United, and was the on-air commentator for the tie at Stoke. I didn't report on the quarter-final but was with Radio WM at the semi-final and final.

After the goalless result at Boundary Park the Sky Blues youth team again drew, this time 1-1 at Highfield Road with Oldham Athletic after extra time, Steve Livingstone on the scoresheet. Three days later they returned to the north-west and the artificial pitch for the second replay where goals from Michael Cook (pen) and Howard Clark secured a 2-1 win and a quarter-final trip to Watford.

Coventry Evening Telegraph, Monday 9 March 1987:

Dynamic midfield man Dean Emerson is touch and go for the FA Cup quarter-final at Hillsborough on Saturday. His chances of playing in Coventry City's biggest game of the season rest on the verdict of a specialist tomorrow. He has remained behind in Coventry for treatment while a 15-strong squad have gone to Bournemouth to start their preparations for the cup-tie. They return on Wednesday night. Emerson said, 'At the moment of impact it felt as though something snapped inside the knee and there was a lot of pain. But when it started to settle it didn't seem as bad. I'll just have to wait and see what the specialist says.'

DEAN EMERSON: When they operated a piece of bone had come off the kneecap. I've got no malice towards Gary Megson whatsoever, it was just an accident. After I had the operation there was a problem with it, I'd been in for five days then they had to do something else so I was back in for a further five. After the first one I was in so much pain they had to operate again, that's what kept me out for the length of time I was away. When I came out of hospital all the leg muscle had wasted away around the knee. I knew it wasn't going to be a quick fix. In the papers they kept saying I'd be back for the semi-final but it was never going to happen. In my mind I was looking at the start of next season but even that didn't happen so I missed the Charity Shield too. Over the next year I was at Lilleshall, the sports injury clinic, for around ten months, on and off, in rehabilitation.

Another 400 tickets

The Sky Blues are being given another 400 seats for the FA Cup tie at Hillsborough. Secretary Graham Hover said today, 'Sheffield have apparently moved a few of their own season-ticket holders to another section of the ground which has enabled them to send us an extra 400 seats for the West Stand. That's where all our fans will be. If we sell these 400 we will have a total following of 14,700 fans on Saturday. It's tremendous.'

The fixtures came thick and fast for Mick Coop's youth team as they travelled to Vicarage Road, Watford, for the last-eight clash. Against a team that included David James and Tim Sherwood and who would win the trophy the following season, a 2-0 victory was secured thanks to Michael Cook and Steve Livingstone.

BOB HALL: After the trip to Spain prior to the Bolton tie, both parties – Coventry City and ITV – agreed I should accompany them ahead of all their ties. Down in Bournemouth, during an impromptu game of football on the beach, as the tide rolled in, George Curtis said the players adjudged worst in training would go into the sea. It was March and cold enough for thermals. Everyone suddenly stepped up a gear, George and John decided that among others Dave Bennett was a candidate. He and others ran for safety, George cried out they were a bunch of softies (or words to that effect).

One anonymous voice then shouted, 'Okay then, you go in!' He didn't pause, stripped off to his pants and ran at speed into the water as though he was in the Caribbean in high summer. The players were in awe but wisely sprinted for the bus. Trainer George Dalton waited stoically with George's clothes and towels while we filmed from a distance.

Coventry Evening Telegraph, Saturday 14 March 1987:

Up for the cup: 15,000 people travel

CITY FANS HIT SKY BLUE ROAD

An army of soccer supporters hit the Sky Blue road today and flooded north, intent on cheering Coventry City into their first FA Cup semi-final this afternoon. Thousands of fans boarded trains, coaches and cars for the 80-mile trip to Sheffield for one of the most crucial games in the club's history.

Coventry railway station was besieged as hundreds tried to cram on to three football specials. It was the same amazing scene at Pool Meadow where dozens of coaches were laid on. The M1 route was a constant stream of coaches and cars showing the sky blue colours.

Sheffield Wednesday Matchday Programme, Saturday 14 March 1987:

HOWARD WILKINSON (Sheffield Wednesday manager): 'A warm welcome to Coventry's travelling band of 14,000 supporters. I'm sure you'll contribute to a fantastic atmosphere at this afternoon's quarter-final. Today is the tenth quarter-final we've played in the last three and a half years, without exception they've generated tremendous atmosphere and tension. There is no doubt in my mind that the experience gained in matches of this nature serves you well. Your unflagging support is essential. We have home advantage, let's all make sure we press it home.'

GARY SHELTON (Sheffield Wednesday midfielder who was in the beaten semi-final sides of 1983 and 1986): 'It would be nice to make it third time lucky but we all know how hard this game against Coventry is going to be. Things have been going well for them, not so well for us in the league.

We're a good cup side, in the cup anything can happen and it should be an interesting game.'

The last time Sheffield Wednesday had lost an FA Cup match at home was in 1973, 14 years and 23 ties ago, against Chelsea.

City: Steve Ogrizovic; Brian Borrows, Brian Kilcline, Trevor Peake, Greg Downs; Dave Bennett, Lloyd McGrath, David Phillips, Nick Pickering; Cyrille Regis, Keith Houchen. Subs: Steve Sedgley, Michael Gynn.

Wednesday: Martin Hodge; Mel Sterland, Mark Smith, Lawrie Madden, Nigel Worthington, Glynn Snodin; Brian Marwood, Gary Megson, Gary Shelton; Lee Chapman, Carl Bradshaw. Subs: David Hirst, Chris Morris.

Referee: Allan Gunn (Sussex).

Coventry Evening Telegraph, Monday 16 March 1987:

NEXT STOP PARADISE!

Sheff Wed 1 (Megson 66) Coventry City 3 (Regis 16, Houchen 78, 83) Att: 48,005

FOULGER MATCH FILE: 'Not since City clinched promotion to the First Division 20 years ago has there been a day of such jubilation and celebration. A record following of nearly 15,000 fans – more than the Highfield Road average gate – made the trip. They were neither disappointed nor let down in any way on a magical and historic day.'

NEVILLE FOULGER: I knew before the quarter-final I would be leaving the *Coventry Evening Telegraph*. The quarter-final was a terrific game and a terrific performance. It was the sort of game that sent shivers down your spine. Hillsborough that day had a packed Kop end with a sea of sky blue at the other end. I've always thought it was one of the great grounds, a proper ground with terraces and the huge Kop. It was a tingling game, to win 3-1, there were wild celebrations afterwards because you're in the semi-finals for the first time ever. The feeling around Coventry was that people couldn't really believe it was all happening. You were pinching yourself, as I knew I was leaving the game was extra special and I was then able to delay my departure to see the season through.

JOHN SILLETT: When I took the job I was quoted as saying that we will win the cup this year – hand on my heart. I looked at the records and we'd never lost the Leamington Hospital Cup! The headline in the paper read 'Sillett: We'll win the FA Cup!' When the games started to go I thought the draw was very cruel to us, only one home tie, but the one place I wanted to go was Hillsborough – the worst game I had as a player was for Chelsea at Sheffield Wednesday. I gave away a penalty and it cost Chelsea dearly. We were going well at the time.

When I walked on to the pitch prior to the quarter-final, you expect your normal following, we saw the massed ranks and thought, 'This is going to be some game, we've got a following here today.'

CYRILLE REGIS: The quarter-final, semi-final and final stand out for me. The Stoke game we didn't play well and managed to scrape through along with the scruffy goal at Old Trafford. The unity of sport at Coventry was the best I've known as a footballer and I've played in some great teams. At West Brom it was a technically better side while with Villa we came second in the league under Ron Atkinson. Our unique selling point was team spirit. That was all fostered by John Sillett who maintained and improved it, we spent more time with each other than our wives and girlfriends. Sill was a great motivator, full of stature, that's one thing about good managers, they know what to say at the right time, an arm around the shoulder to pick the right time to speak to a player – a good man-manager.

DAVE BENNETT: We expected a hostile reception as they were going well at the time, doing well in the league. Hillsborough was a ground we enjoyed playing at as we always got a result. The way we played the first half, we scored a great goal, a terrific move between the 'Three Degrees' (me, Lloyd and Cyrille)! It was a tremendous strike by Cyrille and that set us up and gave us something to fight for. When they did score the roof nearly came off and John was just about to change it when Keith worked his magic. We wanted to come back to Highfield Road at 1-1, we thought we could beat them there so would have settled for a draw.

STEVE OGRIZOVIC: Hillsborough ended up being my favourite ground. Up until the mid-1990s we always got good results there and I always felt I performed well there as well as scoring a goal there earlier in the season. They were a good side back then, very well established in the First Division with some good players. We weren't favourites that day, the atmosphere was terrific and it was a great game notable for Keith Houchen again. We were defending the Kop end and, when Megson equalised, a team that wasn't as strong as we were mentally would have gone under but we didn't. As we did at Wembley, we were like, 'We've lost a goal, let's get back to playing.' The way we came back to turn the momentum around was fantastic.

TREVOR PEAKE: It was incredible to see the City following and inspiring too, it gave us an extra edge, it's times like that you really appreciate the fact that people (coming from Nuneaton, as this run was building up on Sundays I used to go to the local pub where it would be talked about) in that day and age spent a lot of money and a lot of time of their weekends to support you on what had previously been unsuccessful trips. That flashes through your mind, the effort fans make, you really do appreciate it. I was surprised how many people from Nuneaton had made the journeys.

GREG DOWNS: The only half-decent pitch we played on, except for Wembley, was Sheffield Wednesday in the quarter-final. We rode our luck a bit but showed what a good side we were. To be fair to Keith Houchen the finishing at the end was clinical. I still say now it's amazing when you see pictures of the City crowd. It was an overcast day, a perfect one for football, the atmosphere was absolutely rocking, we made hard work of it going one up and then they levelled just after half-time. Even though they had pressed they didn't create a great deal of chances, the back four had stayed the same throughout the run and that helped – we had confidence in each other. The Kop, which we defended second-half, was hugely intimidating, more so than the Stretford End.

NICK PICKERING: This was one of the great days. Fifteen thousand fans there, nearly 50,000 in the ground, it was absolutely fantastic to see Keith score two goals late on. I remember Keith saying at 1-1, with half an hour to go, 'Let's try and get out of here with a draw.' He just took off. It's a magical ground, Sunderland won there in the 1973 semi-final en route to Wembley against Arsenal when I was nine. It was a lucky ground for Coventry, back in the October, the day Oggy scored I was playing left-wing on a really windy day. He's kicked the ball and I turned away because I thought he'd kicked it too far, next thing I look up and the ball is in the net and there's Oggy celebrating!

DAVID PHILLIPS: Hillsborough was always notorious for creating a fantastic atmosphere, I'd played there before, it was a good stamping ground for me and, even after the quarter-final and semi-final, it still proved to be a good ground for me. The amount of Coventry supporters was brilliant, it created a great atmosphere, sky blue and white everywhere. It was a phenomenal attendance, at that time it was a great memory – the noise at Sheffield in general cannot be recreated at many grounds. The quarter-final and semi-final were better than Wembley for this.

BRIAN BORROWS: It was a fantastic atmosphere and we'd always done well there, it was one of our luckiest grounds. At 1-1 we were playing well and still believed we could go on and win the game.

LLOYD McGRATH: I went off injured just before they levelled, the night before I'd been involved in a car crash when I'd been to see Dean Emerson in hospital. I was fine to play, just a bit shaken at the time. John was about to take off Keith Houchen and then, all of a sudden, he's scored twice! The City following that day was tremendous, it was unbelievable seeing so many fans and the noise they made. We didn't have home crowds as high as the support that day at Hillsborough.

KEITH HOUCHEN: When we went to Hillsborough in the quarter-final it's the noise in the place I remember more than anything, more so than Wembley, it nearly lifted you off your feet. When Megson equalised the huge Kop lifted the roof, an incredible roar, but then we ended up winning it comfortably. I'd been a professional since I was 17 but it had all been at the hard working end of the leagues, learning my trade, no glamour at all. The whole occasion made the hairs stand up on the back of your neck, it was just incredible. After I got my second to make it 3-1 and drilled it into the far corner I went and kneeled down in front of the crowd, you could see people crying, laughing, a whole range of emotions which is what sport is all about.

STEVE SEDGLEY: They were all tough away trips, we certainly didn't do it the easy way. You get through and you're waiting for the next one. Hillsborough's a great old ground and the fans made a right old racket, as they did at Stoke. You start to believe you've got half a chance at this stage, in those days the FA Cup was so well renowned you just wanted to go out and do well, do yourself justice. We had a good side and held our own in the First Division, we had players who could win us games but you also needed a bit of luck along the way. At 18 you have no fear, you're quite confident in your own ability and you're playing in an experienced side that is playing well. I'm sure I did have nerves going on at such a crucial time in the game [on 64 minutes when Lloyd McGrath went off injured, Gary Megson then levelled on 66 minutes] but I was just itching to get on and was probably being a right pest to John Sillett saying, 'Get me on!'

STEVE COCKRILL: I was in the dugout again next to the boss. When you watch the highlights on *Match of the Day* there's shots of me sat there, when my mates see it on TV they call me every time, they find it hilarious. I remember Keith Houchen was about to get pulled but John Sillett kept him on a bit longer and look what happened!

STEVE LEE: At the time I was a sports reporter/presenter for *Midlands Today* and also did work for other BBC programmes like *Football Focus.* It was just an average FA Cup run for me up until the trip to Hillsborough. The one I really remember en route to the final was this clash. Coventry took 15,000 supporters and it was memorable because, for what I think, is still the best FA Cup goal I've seen, which was Cyrille Regis when he took a short pass from Dave Bennett just inside the Wednesday half and sprinted away towards the Hillsborough Kop which was full to capacity that day and he scored the most amazing goal, the shot virtually took the net off. I remember Martin Swain in the press box, a Coventry kid, jumped up which you don't generally do, it was such an amazing goal. That gave Coventry so much confidence.

ANDY TURNER: I cut a lone figure in my replica City shirt in the Leeds University refectory where, unbeknown to me and insignificant at that stage, lurked an avid Spurs fan. I didn't jump on the bandwagon until the quarter-finals, and that first glorious trip to Hillsborough knowing, of course, that ticket stubs could be critical in the event that the Sky Blues progressed further.

Travelling with my dad and best mate Michael to join a 15,000-strong contingent of George and John's Sky Blue Army, the M1 was awash with scarves flying from car windows. The match itself was a nervous affair, Gary Megson cancelling out big Cyrille's early advantage before 'Roy of the Rovers' stamped his mark on the competition with two goals in the space of five minutes to spark the celebrations and book City's passage to the semis.

ALAN BIGGS: At the time I was a freelance reporter for the national and local media and wrote an article for the Owls' matchday programme. There was something about Coventry and Sheffield Wednesday that season. They met twice at Hillsborough, including the quarter-final, and it's more the first match that lodges in my memory. That was a 2-2 league draw in October 1986. I spent the whole day at Hillsborough having been commissioned to present a behind-the-scenes video on the Owls. As part of this, I interviewed a happy, smiling goalkeeper in Martin Hodge some hours before kick-off. Little did either of us realise that it was to be the day when the normally reliable Wednesday custodian would be sensationally beaten by his opposite number Steve Ogrizovic. Now Oggy, who'd previously played for my team Chesterfield, was a fairly prodigious kicker of a football. Combine that with a gusty wind blowing from behind his goal at the Leppings Lane End and this particular kick bounced and sailed over the head of the unsuspecting Hodge who was left to walk back in a daze to retrieve the ball from his net.

'Hodgey' was out of luck again for the cup quarter-final as I recall. Only this time there was no blame attached. The key goal in Coventry's 3-1 win was the second, scored with the match level at 1-1 after Gary Megson had replied to Cyrille Regis's early strike. Keith Houchen, as so often that season, was the man of the moment for the Sky Blues. No one begrudged him his match-winning honours or his subsequent Wembley glory but this was maybe the day that defined his destiny. Everyone in sport needs a slice of luck and Houchen got it at Hillsborough with a shot that wickedly deflected off the outstretched leg of Owls defender Mark Smith to give Hodge no chance. Mind you, it was a great foraging run from Houchen that put him in position for the shot. Later, he capitalised on a rare error from another of Howard Wilkinson's 'Mr Reliables', Nigel Worthington, to clinch victory at 3-1, and what a great finish this was, too.

It registered as a shock result, even if the league placings indicated otherwise. With a crowd of 48,000 in the stadium, Wednesday were highly fancied, especially when Megson equalised after the break. On reflection, the powers of Wilkinson's team were on the wane at this time. In previous seasons they had finished high in the top flight, maintaining the momentum of their promotion in 1984 [the same season they defeated Coventry 3-2 in the

FA Cup fourth round at Hillsborough] but a lack of funds for strengthening – the old, familiar story – caught up with them. High octane energy could only go so far. Wilko was shortly to leave for Leeds, somewhat disillusioned by the fact the Hillsborough board allowed him to be approached by a Yorkshire rival club who were then a division lower.

But back to March 1987 and one player who caught my eye that day was Coventry winger Dave Bennett, later to become a Ron Atkinson signing for the Owls. Oh, and I remember the semi-final as well. Where was it played? Hillsborough, of course. As I say there was something about Sheffield Wednesday that year.

IAN WOODS: Mercia Sound didn't need me for the quarter-final at Sheffield Wednesday as Mike and Stuart Linnell presented the whole programme from the ground so, once again, I could just be a fan. Neil White and I joined the 15,000 other Sky Blue fans in the Leppings Lane End. The joy we shared that day was in stark contrast to what happened to Liverpool fans two years later. We stood on the terraces and sang our hearts out. We surged forward as first Regis, then Houchen got the goals to win the tie 3-1. How we loved it that we could clearly be seen in a picture of the fans printed in the *Coventry Evening Telegraph* on the Monday. My main memory of the match, apart from the goals, was getting back to the car and tuning into the Sheffield local radio station. A fan was on the phone sounding off about how it was a disgrace that Wednesday lost to 'Coventry bloody City' in a thick Yorkshire accent. How we laughed and that comment was much imitated in the following years.

NEIL WHITE: Ian Woods, Steve Dimmock and I stood together on Leppings Lane and moved to the side of the lower area to avoid the crush, two years before the disaster which killed so many fans. It was City's best display of the cup run and they deserved the lead through Cyrille but when Megson equalised, we, being ever pessimistic City fans, feared the worst. We reckoned City needed fresh legs and pleaded with Sillett to bring off Houchen who had, frankly, looked out of place for much of the season. Indeed, he became the subject of more and more ire until he went on a devastating second-half run, to put us into the lead. Of course, he went on to grab another and the scenes after the game were manic because we had never reached an FA Cup semi-final before.

JIM BROWN: The Hillsborough quarter-final was something special and is in my top five City games of all time. It was a miserably wet day and I remember dropping my wife in Sheffield to 'do the shops' before heading towards the ground. Parking was difficult but eventually I took my place with friends from the London Supporters' Club in the stand at the Leppings Lane End. The atmosphere was superb and got even better when Cyrille scored a superb opener at the far end. We matched a strong Wednesday side until Gary Megson equalised midway through the second half. Then I thought we would collapse under the Owls pressure but incredibly Houchen netted twice in the last 12 minutes to end Wednesday's 23-match unbeaten home record in the FA Cup. That evening we had been invited out to dinner with some friends and I arrived late and buzzing from the result. At some stage my wife told me to shut up about the football.

A few weeks later I discovered that the dinner had been an informal interview for a job. Somehow I had passed the test and got the job offer a few days after Wembley.

MATT PARTRIDGE: I had been suspended from school so I was banned from going to the quarter-final by my mum but I went anyway! I started my paper round early, got my essentials for the day, and hid round my mate Tom Lancaster's house until we made a run for Coventry station – military precision! We got the train with more friends up to Wadsley Bridge and then on to Hillsborough. The game was absolutely immense. In the Leppings Lane End with many a sky blue fan and making more noise than I can ever remember us making. Great move on the halfway line by Benno and Cyrille and then 'Big C' ran off into the distance. I remember his foot going back and then the roar of the City fans, top drawer sky blue quality! Second half, City were a bit more cagey, Megson hit a shot and it went in at their Kop end, the sound coming from there was deafening! I remember thinking typical City but then super Keith picked up the ball and smashed it off Mark Smith to wrong-foot Martin Hodge and put us back in front. Total jackpot! What seemed like minutes later big Keith controlled the ball on his neck and slid it past Hodge again, he went down on his knees in front of us and the fans went mental, absolute mayhem! I'm getting goosebumps writing it now!

BLAKE WAUGH: Apart from the final this was our best performance of the cup run. I was in the Leppings Lane terrace with my brother and Dad, Mick, and can recall how cramped it was in there. Cyrille's goal was a cracking strike and then came the Houchen show to win 3-1 on a brilliant day.

MIKE YOUNG: I was living and working in Nottingham and travelled with a colleague, another City fan, up to Sheffield. All the roads around the ground were jammed and we didn't think we'd make it in time. We parked miles away and walked in, with retrospect you could see why things went wrong in 1989. We stood in one of the corners at the top of the Leppings Lane End and my anecdote is when Cyrille scored people's arms went up in celebration and knocked my glasses off (I'm pretty short-sighted). In slow motion, in the middle of the celebration, I can picture my glasses arching up into the sky and coming down into the mass of fans. I remember thinking I wasn't going to see the rest of the game never mind find my way home! I cried out 'STOP!' and, to their credit, all the fans around actually did seem to stop as I cried, 'My glasses, my glasses!' I found them intact on the floor under all those feet. That was the lucky omen for me and Big Cyrille's goal was a big moment.

ROB SUMMERFIELD: Three rounds in, being clad in black, no CCFC club colours. I'm not usually superstitious but the thought occurred wearing a scarf could bring bad luck. Ridiculous, but the Sky Blue man in black made his way to Yorkshire. We went by car, again, were late into the ground and the sheer number of bodies persuaded us to stand by the corner flag. Just two years later the image of how packed the Leppings Lane End was took on a new horrific meaning. It's something, the 'could have been us feeling', that has always lived with me. City were tremendous that day, Regis and Bennett were unplayable on the break. Wednesday had a decent full-back, Mel Sterland, who made several impressive first-half forays up the wing. A lot of Coventry sides over the years would have buckled but there was a kind of communication between the team and supporters, when they were low we sang harder and when we were quiet they lifted us. I thought 3-1 was about right, it was rarely in doubt.

MOZ BAKER: I went to Hillsborough with my now wife, we moved three or four times during the game because I didn't feel safe. We went originally into the central area behind the goal and it was far too busy. We then went out to the corner part and then ended up right in the top corner. When we scored the third goal there was a real surge and I know my wife was really quite scared. She hadn't been to many games and that kind of took the edge off it for me. It was an amazing following and a great day but that was scary, far too crowded for comfort.

DANNY FINLAY: My main memory of that day is how packed it was on the terrace. I remember my dad saying that he was trying to hold on to me as his feet were off the floor. We were around to the left-hand side and when we scored he was trying to keep hold of me with his feet off the concrete steps.

DEAN NELSON: I queued for my ticket at Highfield Road for the quarter-final, interest was high as we'd never been past the sixth round. I went to Pool Meadow bus station to get a Harry Shaw CCFC coach pass which enabled me to travel to the match. This would be the only time in my supporting of the team that I had travelled to an away match by coach and I've never done it since. We were all at the Leppings Lane End, I was down by the corner flag so wasn't too squashed. I met some old schoolmates from Bulkington who I'd not seen for 12 years, we'd always talked about getting to Wembley as kids, now it was within our sights. The game went so fast all I can remember was coming out of the ground and looking for the number of the coach which was mine, it seemed like there was hundreds of them all lined up. I got back to Bulkington in time to watch Tony Gubba's commentary on *Match of the Day* and Jimmy Hill grinning from ear to ear.

ANDY SCAYSBROOK: The next round we were drawn away at Hillsborough, my favourite away ground. 15,000 City fans travelled and my mates and I kept up our pact of travelling together but this time we were convinced that if we didn't we would be knocked out and thousands of City fans would be baying for our blood! It's funny how superstition plays such a vital role in the make-up of the football fan. What a day, what a game that was. My memory of Cyrille breaking from the halfway line and lashing in that goal is as clear today as it ever was. The Leppings Lane End that would sadly become a scene of death and destruction two years later was a bouncing mass of City fans singing like we were world champions.

I remember when Houch smashed in the second of his goals right in front of us and fell to his knees with arms wide open in salutation to the City faithful as the Leppings Lane erupted into scenes of total mass celebration. I had never witnessed such scenes before and I can honestly remember having a huge lump in my throat and I'm not too proud to admit that there was a tear in my eye and I wasn't the only one. Grown men were hugging complete strangers, we were singing at the top of our voices and the sense of unity and family was something that will stay with me forever.

That night we got very drunk. The dream was getting closer and we knew it, we dared to believe now and you couldn't contain the expectation. The team were magnificent, 11 players scrapping for their lives, urged on by the Sky Blue masses as wave upon wave of support flowed off the terraces and into the players' hearts to help drive us on. Surely, this year, no one could stop us?

KEV MONKS: I had a ticket in the terrace at Hillsborough. We got into the ground around 2.15pm and joined the queues of City supporters trying to get in. Once inside, the City fans were funnelled through an entrance that led on to the Leppings Lane terrace. There were more entrances but these were not made clear and everyone started packing on to the terrace. I got halfway down the terrace behind the goal and looked around. I could see people everywhere but no sign of the people I had travelled with or any of my mates. I decided the safest thing to do was to wedge my feet in the railings halfway down, so I had not only a good view of the goal but of their Kop end also. As kick-off time approached the crush got worse and worse and I was shoved hard up against the fence which I was now clinging on to with both arms for dear life. Supporters were climbing into the stand and I counted about thirty who decided that getting out of the terrace was the best option.

Unable to even put my hands in my pockets, I stood side on to the game, hoping the match would fly past as soon as possible and I could escape from this torment with my life intact. It was the same with others I spoke to and even the goal celebrations in a 3-1 win were pretty muted to what they would have been on a half-full terrace. I shouted 'Yes!' as I walked out of the ground although in a fair bit of pain due to people pressing against my spine all afternoon. Like many others, I was not only celebrating Coventry City had now gone further in the FA Cup than ever before but I was alive to tell the tale.

LEE CORDEN: The first seed of doubt that we might not get to Wembley was sowed at Hillsborough as we stood in the Leppings Lane End. I remember how tightly we were packed into each pen but felt safe enough because, as a nine-year-old, you don't know any different. When Gary Megson drew Wednesday level after big Cyrille's first-half goal, I suddenly thought it might not happen for us. Perhaps we could be beaten? As you look back nearly 30 years on, it's easy to remember the TV pictures you've seen over and over rather than the real-life image but, just like Gynn's goal at Stoke, I can still see Houchen's efforts crossing the line in front of me and my dad protecting me from the surge of the crowd.

NEIL JONES: Sheffield Wednesday was a great day. My mum and dad had friends in Sheffield and we stayed up there but I can honestly say two things stand out for me, the atmosphere and that Cyrille Regis (to me as a five-year-old) looked like He-Man, the children's cartoon of the time, just pure power.

BOB EALES: I was still at sea, there was a sense of pride at the club getting to a semi-final for the first time in their history, an achievement we'll probably never see happen again.

STEVE & HEATHER TAYLOR: By the end of December 1986 Heather was convinced the Sky Blues had the spirit and talent to win the next FA Cup. Having lived through the 1967 promotion to Division One she recognised the signs. You have to understand that Heather has sky blue blood and I had also had a transfusion! She said to me, 'I'm going to start writing an FA Cup song for us.' I just looked bewildered and said, 'Why?' but Heather has a sixth sense for these sorts of things! The song went well and was duly demoed by me. 'Go For It City' was born! It was presented to the club just after the sixth-round win against Sheffield Wednesday who had engaged an agent by the name of Joe Stainer for the occasion. He liked the song and asked how we were going to go about recording and distributing it. Well, having been told by Vic Lanzer at EMI that the song was great but Coventry City didn't have sufficient gates to warrant them getting involved, Heather said Coventry City deserve a cup song as much as the big clubs so we'll do it all ourselves. No mean feat that, especially when all you have is a small bedroom studio in an ex-coal board semi-detached in Keresley Village. Joe agreed and it was decided that if the Sky Blues got through the semi-final they would descend on the Taylors at their house and record the song.

The remaining three ties saw the 'Crazy Gang' depart thanks to two sublime strikes from Glenn Hoddle and Chris Waddle in Tottenham's 2-0 triumph at Plough Lane. Second Division Leeds won 2-0 at third tier Wigan

Athletic, former Sky Blue Micky Adams clinching the win with a fine strike from range – with his right foot, while there was huge controversy at Highbury. Arsenal trailed Graham Taylor's Watford 2-1 with minutes to play when a long throw was launched into the Hornets' penalty area for the head of Niall Quinn.

Watford centre-half Steve Sims jumped with the Irishman and appeared to climb on his back, a fact noted by the linesman who flagged immediately. Referee Brian Stevens let play continue, Watford counter-attacked and Luther Blissett sealed the win in front of the famous Clock End. Arsenal, as you can imagine, were up in arms about the decision and insisted Stevens consult his linesman. After a brief consultation the official awarded the goal and Watford joined Tottenham, Leeds and Coventry in the FA Cup semi-finals.

Coventry Evening Telegraph, Monday 16 March 1987:

IT'S LEEDS – and fans love it

CUP-CRAZY CITY GOES WILD

Coventry was cock-a-hoop on an all-time soccer high this afternoon. Jubilant Sky Blues fans were ready to cheer their side all the way to an FA Cup Final at Wembley. The city was glued to radio sets to hear the semi-final draw pitch them into battle with Leeds. Today the Sky Blues rocket still hadn't come down to earth from the dizzy heights of Saturday's thrilling triumph in the quarter-final at Sheffield Wednesday. Everyone had a spring in their step and a smile on their face. And all the talk was of Saturday's historic triumph.

At Highfield Road, telephones and tills in the Sky Blues shop were ringing non-stop. Secretary Graham Hover said, 'It has gone mad. There's a tremendous amount of interest and it's not surprising. Coventry has waited a long time for this.' The mood in workplaces all over the city was ecstatic and factory floors buzzed with cup-run talk while, in pubs and clubs, City's chances became the only topic of conversation.

Ex-City star Jim Holton, now landlord of the Rising Sun in Spon Street, said, 'Everybody is thrilled. It's good for the city and it's got everybody going. Coventry supporters haven't had a great deal of success for a long time, so it's fantastic for them.'

The Sky Blues, 50/1 outsiders at the beginning of the cup run, were made 5/2 second favourites. Tottenham led the way at 11/8 with Watford 100/30 and Leeds 5/1.

In celebration the Co-op reduced prices across its stores. A four pack of Harp Lager (£1.69), 20 Lambert and Butlers (£1.26), 20 John Player Specials (£1.34), 99 Tea Bags (37p), Cream Crackers (18p) and a bottle of HP Sauce (39p) were among the bargains available to the people of Coventry.

STEVE LEE: I remember going to Ryton for the semi-final draw and there were big names as possible opponents. When Coventry drew Second Division Leeds the players all whooped and apparently it went down badly with Leeds who were determined to prove them wrong and give them a hard game.

ANDY SCAYSBROOK: When the draw was made for the semi-final I was with my mate Andy, we listened in on the radio at lunchtime. We didn't care who we got because at this point we knew we could beat anybody and that was the feeling by this time. In our minds we were entering the world-beating stage, us, Coventry City. It was hard to fathom but the mindset at the time was one that has never been equalled before. Every game we went to we were expecting to win and were on a roll. I can remember the announcer as the balls were drawn, 'Tottenham Hotspur will play Watford' and we leapt up into the air!

Leeds was seen as the easier draw. 'We're the famous Coventry City and we're going to Wembley, Wembley!' We sang it loud and proud, I'm not sure what the neighbours thought but who cared, we were living the dream. City in the semi-final of the FA Cup, one game away from our first ever appearance at Wembley was something we could only ever dream of. It still feels like a dream, even today.

BRIAN BORROWS: We were more than happy when we were drawn to play again at Hillsborough. Leeds probably felt, along with us, that they had the best draw. We certainly didn't think it was going to be easy but it was a more favourable draw away from Tottenham and

Watford for a game we knew we could win if we played to our potential.

JOHN POYNTON: When the semi-final draw was made it couldn't have been better for us. We were better off playing an established side rather than against Watford who had only been in Division One for five seasons under Graham Taylor with Elton John.

Coventry Evening Telegraph, Tuesday 17 March 1987:

Attend Oxford game and you get ticket – Cup pledge to Sky Blue fans

FA Cup marvels Coventry City today guaranteed a semi-final ticket to every fan who attends Friday night's match against Oxford at Highfield Road. The promise became possible when the Sky Blues were unexpectedly allocated a staggering 29,000 tickets for the clash with Leeds United at Hillsborough. That's more than the Highfield Road capacity of around 27,500. Originally, City had expected approximately 22,000 tickets which would have been the normal share of the ground capacity of 54,000. But the FA today decided that, for safety reasons, only the two competing clubs should have tickets. Host club Sheffield Wednesday won't be selling any.

The FA then ruled that Sky Blues fans be given the massive Hillsborough Kop – the biggest in the country. It was enlarged and given a £1m roof this season and can now accommodate 21,000 people. City are also being allocated the Main Stand which seats another 8,000. This guarantees total segregation of rival supporters – something about which the FA were deeply concerned.

CUP-TIE SHOCK – IT'S SUNDAY

Leeds crowd aggro fear forces move

Coventry City's FA Cup semi-final clash with Leeds will be played on a Sunday. The dramatic switch was ordered today because of the threat of violence in an expected 54,000 strong crowd. It has been moved from 11 April to 12 April – with a 12.15pm kick-off.

Police advised it and the Football Association agreed. The fixture will be played at Hillsborough, where Sheffield Wednesday chairman Bert McGee said today, 'The police wanted to ensure there is as little trouble in the stadium as possible. At 12.15pm on a Sunday there should be no drinking.'

It will certainly be the biggest police presence for a game at Hillsborough and may become the largest mounted for a domestic fixture in England. The cost will run into tens of thousands of pounds and will be set against gate receipts.

Coventry City secretary Graham Hover said: 'There is nothing we can do about it. We have been told we have got to play on Sunday and we just have to accept that decision and get on with it. The sad thing is that it is yet another victory for the hooligan element.'

ANDY SCAYSBROOK: My friend, Tony Golding, a big City fan who I had worked with at John Wright Photography – we both left on the same day, me to start my freelance business, him to cycle to Morocco – had been away and missed all of the drama. Remember, this was before mobile phones. He had written to tell me he'd seen an English newspaper in Algeria and read with astonishment the headline 'Yorkshire Police launch biggest ever Police operation to segregate fans before the FA Cup semi-final between Coventry and Leeds'. I could tell in his writing how shocked and surprised he was and to find out in such a way must have only heightened his excitement – 'I'm coming back mate, see you at Wembley!' The paper was a week old so he had a lot of travelling to get back home, especially as he was on a mountain bike!

Three days later Oxford United visited Highfield Road as 23,924 packed into the great old stadium to ensure they had a ticket for Leeds. Goalless at half-time, the Sky Blues turned on the style attacking the West End as first, Dave Bennett danced past defenders to score from an improbable angle and then a brace from Cyrille Regis saw City maintain eighth place in the First Division. Including cup games it was a sixth successive win, a post-war record, watched by the biggest league attendance for six years.

Coventry City Matchday Programme, Friday 20 March 1987:

Trevor Peake, 'I can understand people talking about those days when the club was winning trophies and about the League Cup semi-final matches against West Ham United. After all, until now, they were just about the most successful times at the club in 20 years or so. It would be nice for us to be the team of the 1980s and for supporters 20 years from now to be talking of our success. It would be doubly nice if we could win the cup and finish higher than sixth in the First Division. That really would be something to celebrate.'

FA CUP TICKETS

We have been allocated 29,000 tickets for the FA Cup semi-final match against Leeds United at Hillsborough on Sunday 12 April, kick off 12.15pm. Eight thousand of those tickets are seats in the Main Stand and the remaining 21,000 are for standing on the famous Hillsborough Kop. The seats are priced £12 and £8 and the Kop tickets are £5.

We can assure you that everyone at tonight's match against Oxford United will be able to buy a cup ticket (we cannot guarantee a seat) provided you retain your ticket stub for tonight's game. You must produce a ticket stub for tonight's match to be sure of being able to buy a cup ticket.

ANDY SCAYSBROOK: The surge for tickets had reached an unprecedented level by this time and, as we all had the ticket stubs from the previous games, we got ours easily. Only this time we had a new member of our group, my dad. He could no longer attend regularly as his publican work patterns demanded his attention but he made it to the semi-final. Our little band of brothers that had followed this unravelling fairy tale had a new member and I couldn't think of a better one. Here was the man who had started this love affair for me and now he was going to join us on the trip to Hillsborough. I'm sure the other lads were hoping that the magic spell we had created to get us this far would not be broken by the new addition but, if anyone deserved to be there, it was my dad.

A permanent record of the victory at Sheffield Wednesday was made available to City supporters. Wednesday produced a one-hour video recording of the match which could be purchased for £11 for either VHS or Betamax recorders.

The travelling hordes (15,000) who headed up the M1 to Hillsborough beat by 2,000 the previous record of away supporters who travelled to Wolves in 1973 for the FA Cup quarter-final when City lost 2-0 at Molineux.

The FA Youth Cup semi-final saw Manchester City take on the Sky Blue babes in a two-legged clash. Howard Clark's goal gave Mick Coop's men a 1-0 first-leg lead to take into the return at Maine Road a week later.

City's winning run came crashing to an end at Plough Lane, Wimbledon, as Dave Bassett's men triumphed 2-1 after Michael Gynn gave City an early lead. Just 4,370 watched the fixture, the second-smallest First Division crowd since the war. Two further away games followed in quick succession as the Sky Blues went from 20 March to 20 April without a home fixture. There was a defeat to Aston Villa (1-0) and a goalless draw at the City Ground with Brian Clough's men. Villa hadn't won since Boxing Day and would end the season propping up the league having taken six of their 36 points against City – their only away win of the campaign came at, you've guessed it, Highfield Road. The fixture at Villa Park was notable for local lad Tony Dobson's first-team debut. Most importantly, there were no injuries reported with eight days to go until the titanic clash at Hillsborough against Leeds United.

Manchester City took the FA Youth Cup semi-final to a replay with a 1-0 victory. Paul Lake from the penalty spot took the tie to a third game at Highfield Road.

The Coventry and District Football League cancelled all fixtures on the day of the semi-final. Chairman Alan Richardson said, 'We expect most of our players would want the opportunity of cheering City to Wembley so we have decided to suspend fixtures for the day – even a cup final – because we all want the team to get to Wembley.'

Coventry Evening Telegraph, Monday 6 April 1987:

Clough: City to reach Wembley

Outspoken Nottingham Forest boss Brian Clough is backing Coventry City for Wembley. So is former Sky Blues favourite Stuart Pearce, sold to Forest nearly two years ago.

They have both revealed they will be rooting for City in Sunday's FA Cup semi-final against Leeds United at Hillsborough. Clough said, 'For the sake of Midlands football, I hope City go to Wembley. People have kindly said that we have carried the mantle for the Midlands in recent years but it's nice that a club like Coventry should come along and have some success. Having got so far in the FA Cup, they'll want to go all the way to Wembley and if they do I'll be rooting for them on the big day. Coventry seem to be on the verge of regaining the identity they had 15 or 16 years ago.

'I can vouch for the calibre of George Curtis and John Sillett and the club seem to be moving in the right direction.' Pearce said, 'I really fancy them to beat Leeds – and I sincerely hope they do. I'd love them to go to Wembley and win the FA Cup because they are the club who gave me my big chance. I still have a soft spot for them.'

A packed Main Stand at Highfield Road watched the youth team beat Manchester City 3-0 to take their place in the two-legged final against Charlton Athletic. A double from Steve Livingstone and one from Paul Shepstone defeated the Maine Road men whose line-up included Andy Hinchcliffe, Paul Lake, Paul Warhurst, Jason Beckford and were managed by former City great Tony Book.

GAVIN CLIFTON: I'm 44 now, 17 when we won the cup. There were no mobiles, blogs or message boards in those days. We took the coach to Hillsborough for the semi-final with Leeds United. The pub over the road from Highfield Road, the Mercers Arms, had become a bit of a tentative first watering hole for me and my best mate from school, Kev. It was a very busy local pub with some fantastic characters. We'd somehow managed to secure ourselves tickets to the semi-final and seats on the pub coach trip. The driver was keen to get away but at the front of the coach a large blond fella with a bottle of Bacardi (not breezer) in hand stood up and cried, 'Hey, hang on a minute, it's our Billy, he'll have it!'

And here is where the story begins. Picture this, Billy, a well liked chap who everybody knows who's probably in his early 30s at the time, is having a nice little Sunday morning stroll down the road to get his Sunday paper and a pint of milk. Just enough money for these basic items and he's wearing his slippers. Don't forget there were no mobiles to drop the missus a text and the driver is revving up to get out of town. Next thing, Billy is getting an ovation as he makes the only decision possible when asked, 'Do you want this spare ticket?'

On the coach I remember getting to Walsgrave Hospital and thinking, 'We're not going to get out of Coventry here.' Coach after coach and then word came, 'The police are checking all coaches, no booze!' I've never seen so much booze drank so quick in my life to this day! We were lucky getting to Hillsborough in good time and managed to squeeze ourselves into good positions on the packed Kop as 'Don't You Forget About Me' played on the tannoy system – fantastic! And then the game began.

GEOFF FOSTER: I first went up to Highfield Road in October 1963 and four years of magnificent success followed as the Sky Blue revolution took place. My favourite players were George Hudson, Neil Martin, Ronnie Rees, the incomparable Ian Gibson and so many more. My rugby career at Kenilworth meant I didn't see the ties against Bolton, Manchester United, Stoke and Sheffield Wednesday so Hillsborough for the semi-final was my introduction to the cup run and what a Sunday that was! It was an early start, our coach was departing from The Royal Warwickshire Club just off the ring road at a very early time for the lunchtime kick-off. When we turned the corner we saw loads of coaches waiting and our attention was drawn to a very old single-decker bus. We all thought, 'Pity the poor sods who are going to Hillsborough in that!' You've guessed...that was our coach! Our concerns were ill-placed, however, we made it safely and, despite the huge traffic problems, were safely delivered to the ground.

ROB GURNEY: I had my little black Mini at the time and was giving my dad a lift. On the day there were horrendous traffic problems on the M1 and we got caught up in it. We eventually got into the environs of Hillsborough but way away from the stadium and had to run to the ground.

IAN WOODS: For the semi-final, it was back to working for Mercia Sound. There wasn't room for all of us in the press box so I sat in ordinary seats in the Main Stand with Kirk Stephens while Mike Liggins and Stuart Linnell commentated on the action. We were a couple of rows of seats away from the press benches, there wasn't enough room for us all and they certainly wouldn't give little old

Mercia Sound four tickets for the press area. Kirk and I were with the Coventry fans and it was quite odd sitting there with a radio microphone wearing headphones with a former Sky Blues player but it worked out well because we were able to do a bit of punditry to link the commentary with Mike and Stuart.

IAN BOLTON: I was now with Radio WM and commentated with Paul Franks from the press area.

ROB SUMMERFIELD: I travelled on a coach from the Humber Pub, it was full of lads from the old West End terrace days. All the classic songs rang out but I was nervous, still refusing to wear colours.

MATT PARTRIDGE: School was awash with Sky Blue, Coventry had more fans than I could ever remember! I got the train again with the ever expanding Sky Blue Army, we were dropped in the centre and then took a slow bus to the ground. We were in the Kop end this time.

BLAKE WAUGH: My dad drove us to Hillsborough again with my brother, and cousin Matt. We passed the author on the way up the M1 in our white Cavalier but the car soon overheated which led us to abandon it while it cooled down and then we ran the last couple of miles to the ground. We were at the back of the Kop. The view was awful as the players looked like ants with us stood so high up.

ANDY TURNER: I could hardly believe it when we were drawn against Leeds and another trip to Sheffield. Back on campus it was time for the shirt to go in the drawer and certainly not to be worn about town. It was the 80s after all, a time when football hooliganism was custom and practice at most matches and Leeds fans weren't exactly known for their good-natured banter with opposing supporters. Living in their midst, I preferred to remain anonymous. The journey to Hillsborough had a touch of déjà vu about it but, as three of 29,000 City fans this time, the atmosphere took on an intensity the likes of which we had never seen before – a Sky Blue armada floating on waves of optimism. There were plenty of nerves gnawing away in the pit of your stomach, knowing just how close and yet how far we were from achieving the hitherto impossible dream of a cup final.

But there was also an overriding air of confidence among the players and supporters, taking comfort in John Sillett's bold early claim that City's name was already on the cup. That, coupled with Starship's 'Nothing's Gonna Stop Us Now' flying up the charts.

DEAN NELSON: My girlfriend Debbie, my sister Joy, her husband Paul and I all collected our ticket stubs and coupons and tickets were obtained. On the day we went up the M1 on a bright, sunny, Sunday morning. What a sight greeted us, a mass of Sky Blue on the huge Kop, for sound alone there was only one winner. Six years prior I had been at Upton Park to see City lose the League Cup semi-final to a Second Division side, I hoped it wasn't going to happen again.

ANDY SCAYSBROOK: We travelled up to Hillsborough on the coach and I can remember walking to the ground in the beautiful spring sunshine. The atmosphere among the City fans was electric. Oh how we had dreamed of such greatness, none of us had experienced an FA Cup semi-final before.

KEV MONKS: When the draw was made I cried out, 'Not Hillsborough again.' Some people I know immediately refused to go there again despite City being allocated the Kop plus seating in the Main Stand. It was a day that I moved house but that could wait. I was out of the house by 7.30am and we arrived in Sheffield just after nine. We parked up and got into the ground before 10am for the 12.15pm kick-off. I met my mate, John, someone who died at a young age, who had been so busy organising a coach that he had forgotten his match ticket but, thankfully, the turnstile operator let him in and then told him City would not win.

LEE CORDEN: We were stood in the huge Kop for the semi-final. It was the most electric atmosphere I'd ever experienced at a match and I mistook Leeds for a small club because they were in the Second Division but, when I heard and saw their support, I realised I was wrong.

Mike Liggins joined Mercia Sound after he left Warwick University in 1984. At the beginning of season 1986/87 he began to go home and away with the Sky Blues for Mercia as their lead commentator. Mike and Stuart Linnell provided live commentary and cassette tapes were made available to City supporters from both the semi-final and final. The excerpts in bold type are Mike and Stuart's live commentary from Hillsborough.

MIKE LIGGINS: A very good afternoon and welcome to Hillsborough. The big day has finally arrived, Coventry City's finest hour, in the semi-finals of the FA Cup for the very first time and Leeds United the opposition. As you've heard the kick-off has been delayed. We now have a 12.30pm kick-off because the Leeds team coach broke down, they were late in arriving along with many, many thousands of Coventry City fans struggling to get into Hillsborough due to the traffic chaos in Coventry this morning and then again on the M1.

MIKE LIGGINS: There was a feeling of great excitement, the ground was packed and the Kop full of Sky Blues supporters. John Sillett was a fantastic character, he didn't suffer fools gladly and was a great interview. I've been in the business now for nearly 30 years and, looking back, there are few that can match him for his honesty, humour and ability to deliver a fantastic quote. From a journalistic point of view he was an absolute dream.

STUART LINNELL: The big thing I recall is the late start to the game. We left Coventry past Walsgrave Hospital and out towards the motorway in this convoy of Coventry City cars with scarves, flags, you name it, every time we saw a flag hanging from a house car horns would be sounded in salute and everyone joined in. We were making good time and, as it happened, I'd worked in Sheffield for six years at Hallam FM before moving to Coventry and knew the roads well. We came over the top of a hill and all you could see was red tail lights in front of you. Fortunately, I knew how to get to Hillsborough but we were still pushed for time.

I was with Kirk Stephens and we got there just in time to see the delayed kick-off.

STEVE OGRIZOVIC: Sunday was different, those were the days when you played at 3pm on a Saturday afternoon and anything else was a change to routine. It was a big game, on TV (albeit with an hour time delay on ITV) but it wouldn't have mattered if we had played Saturday, Sunday, Thursday or midnight, everybody was looking forward to the game. The feeling among the players was this was going to be our year and this grew after we beat Stoke. Everyone was convinced we were going to reach Wembley for the first time. We were favourites as Leeds were Second Division and we had to perform as favourites not underdogs. The start was delayed due to the traffic delays around the stadium.

GREG DOWNS: The pitch was rock hard, it was bobbling all over the place in the warm-up. We were down the tunnel ready to go when, ten minutes before kick-off, we got sent back to the dressing room because the crowd weren't all in as the roads around Hillsborough were packed. The lads, who were all prepared and ready to go thought, 'What do we do now?' We all had our matchday routines and were ready to play.

City: Steve Ogrizovic; Brian Borrows, Brian Kilcline, Trevor Peake, Greg Downs; Dave Bennett, David Phillips, Lloyd McGrath, Nick Pickering; Cyrille Regis, Keith Houchen. Subs: Michael Gynn, Steve Sedgley.

Leeds: Mervyn Day, Neil Aspin, Jack Ashurst, Brendan Ormsby, Micky Adams; Andy Ritchie, John Stiles, David Rennie, John Sheridan; Ian Baird, John Pearson. Subs: Peter Haddock, Keith Edwards.

Referee: Roger Milford (Bristol).

TREVOR PEAKE: In the semi-final it was leaning towards Leeds early on and, from when the draw was made, we had smiling faces, it was the best draw we could have hoped for with them in the Second Division and evading Tottenham and Watford. Reality soon bit in the first 15 minutes. They were no mugs. It was a one-off and we were the favourites. We soon realised it wasn't going to be easy.

STUART LINNELL: Adams prepares to take the corner, it's been mostly Leeds United so far, in this first quarter of an hour. Here comes the corner from Adams...and there's the shot, IT'S A GOAL FOR LEEDS UNITED! David Rennie's header at the near post, Adams's corner, Coventry City go behind with only 14 minutes gone of this FA Cup semi-final, Coventry City with it all to do.

MICKY ADAMS: Leeds flew out of the traps at Hillsborough. Coventry made a nervous start and Oggy made two or three saves after David Rennie's header found the net as we piled on the pressure.

CYRILLE REGIS: We went 1-0 down. It was my fault, I should have been marking David Rennie. I had a couple of chances after that and we could have gone two down, Oggy pulled off a couple of good saves. Looking back on it, because Rennie was my man and I let him go, I tried too hard and missed two or three opportunities.

STEVE OGRIZOVIC: I wasn't conscious at the time that the delay had affected us but Leeds flew out of the traps and came at us really quickly, we were really under the cosh and I remember having to make quite a few saves early on. David Rennie then scored, who ironically became my team-mate in years to come, and we managed to hang in there for the first 30 minutes. We then started to get a grip and began to control the game, got on the ball and created chances. A bit like the quarter-final after Megson levelled, you could feel we were getting closer and closer.

KEITH HOUCHEN: We were sleeping early on, we normally defended really well and then you're chasing the game [for the first time in the cup run]. But, we chased it well, were solid and didn't give them anything else. The only danger when you're missing chances is you start getting a bit desperate and go back to front too quickly.

GREG DOWNS: It was hard to get going and, to be fair to Leeds, they flew at us and took control early on. We still missed the best chances though but I had a nightmare, just couldn't get going up against Andy Ritchie.

NICK PICKERING: That game, after the victories at Stoke, Manchester United and Sheffield Wednesday, we were favourites to win and Leeds didn't half come at us in the first 20 minutes. If it wasn't for Oggy we could have been 2-0 down but we also had a couple of chances.

DAVID PHILLIPS: Maybe we were resting on our laurels. Friends of mine were staying in the Leeds team hotel and the fire alarm went off the night before the game, they had to evacuate in the middle of the night. For them it was like a home fixture, it was a case of lets hit them as early as possible and create a decent tempo which is what they did. It put us on the back foot for quite some time but, it's easy with hindsight to say this now, we weren't a side to shirk or fold, the three years I spent at Coventry I don't think we capitulated to anyone. It was very difficult to get to the pace of the game.

ROB GURNEY: As we were late we missed David Rennie's header and I remember, in the days of terracing, just clinging on with my dad in the Kop.

GAVIN CLIFTON: The main thing that stood out for me in the semi-final was the wall of noise created by the Leeds fans when David Rennie (City legend) scored that first goal, I'd never experienced anything like it before. The game ticked away with Houchen the best hold-up man since Dick Turpin.

NEIL WHITE: 'Woodsie' was involved in radio duties for the semi-final but I insisted Steve join us for some more because he had now become our lucky omen. For the first time my girlfriend, Andi, joined us, not that she saw much of the game because her contact lens got stuck in the back of her eyeball but the game was nervy and exciting.

MATT PARTRIDGE: In the Kop this time, I remember looking out to a sea of white, Leeds were in town and they were loud! We conceded early and were lucky to keep it to one. We were dire early on.

ROB SUMMERFIELD: It was a cracking game. Leeds were in the old Second Division but you couldn't tell. We were on the Wednesday Kop this time and the atmosphere was tense but wonderful. David Rennie gave them a lead that seemed to last forever, mocking our dreams. Micky Adams was typically good and the script was going wrong. Even at the back we were nervous and there were many spills and scrambles.

LEE CORDEN: When Leeds took the lead and held it until half-time I turned to my dad and burst into tears because, again, I thought the dream was over. He simply reassured me that our name was on the cup this season.

DEAN NELSON: Within a few minutes David Rennie headed Leeds in front, Cyrille had missed a few chances but we continued to battle for every ball.

Half-time: Coventry City 0 Leeds United 1 (Rennie 14) Att: 51,372

JOHN SILLETT: Half-time was the big thing. We kept the dressing room door open deliberately, we were right across the corridor from Leeds. I said, 'Let them hear us sing,' and Lloyd McGrath started to sing, 'Here we go, here we go.'

LLOYD McGRATH: That was crazy. All of the lads looked at John and I and then joined in, it was absolutely fantastic! The noise we made, it gave us a lift because our first-half performance wasn't brilliant but second-half we came out and were well up for the challenge.

CYRILLE REGIS: That was a turning point – it was a spiritual moment, it really was in terms of purpose and ambition, it was incredible. I went in the dressing room and said, 'Sorry boys, it's my fault.' You put your hands up. John Sillett is doing his team talk, a few words, then it went quiet. Suddenly, Lloyd McGrath, who doesn't say a word unless he's had a few beers, started singing, 'Here we go, here we go...' quite lightly and then everybody from players, subs, John Sillett, the kitman [Steve Cockrill], George Dalton the physio – all of us shouted it out at the top of our voices for what seemed like ages but was probably 25 to 30 seconds. It was an amazing moment.

DAVE BENNETT: That was absolutely brilliant! Cyrille came in at half-time and apologised to everyone and then, all of a sudden, Lloyd starts singing! Leeds must have wondered what the hell was going on as it was they who were winning! We're singing at the top of our voices, it was like a battle cry, we got ourselves together and said we're not going to give this up. The last person you would have thought would start singing was Lloyd, it lifted us and we soon got ourselves back in the game. To see the big man, with his experience, down, we needed him, he was a part of the team and this was a group of players that was astonishing in more ways than one. They stuck together and were different class.

JOHN SILLETT: I heard a voice in the Leeds dressing room say, 'They're singing in there.' It was one of those things. You do something silly and it works. It was the first time we had trailed in the cup run.

LLOYD McGRATH: We still had belief. I don't think as a team we'd played that well in the first half, the delayed start didn't help matters as we were really hyped up and the delay drained us a bit. It took us a bit of time to get going. We'd had to calm ourselves down and then build ourselves back up again for when we finally went out. We were confident we could win the game as we'd had some good victories en route to the semi-final.

KEV MONKS: I have never been so down at a game as I was at half-time. Losing 1-0 and to have come this far and go out with a whimper was not on. The booming out of the song 'Live It Up' by Mental as Anything just made things worse.

Former Sky Blues right-back Kirk Stephens had recently retired from the professional game due to a knee injury. Prior to the semi-final he had signed for former City defender Jimmy Holmes at Nuneaton Borough. Kirk joined Ian Woods in the stand at Hillsborough to provide match analysis along with Mike and Stuart in the press box.

KIRK STEPHENS: John Sillett's put Micky on to attack the Leeds back four. He's got that extra bit of pace, I think he'll do a tremendous job. I just hope he can do it in the next few minutes, I really do, to give the City a boost.

JOHN SILLETT: Just before Gynny went on I said to him, 'You've got the quick feet and that's what we're missing.' The ball kept going across the box and nobody could get on the end of it. I said, 'Use your quick feet, get into that box, be sharp, be alive to any little deflection.'

MICHAEL GYNN: I was desperate to get on to the pitch. We were 1-0 down and, to be fair, we didn't look like we were going to score. With my pace I felt I could make a difference to the team and make an impact on the game. To be fair, I remember John saying after the game it was only because Nick Pickering got injured that he actually put me on. In those days you went out, expressed yourself and played your natural game.

NICK PICKERING: That was a massive moment, we're struggling at 1-0 down and I've got this dead leg ten minutes after half-time. I'm not one to go off but I'm really struggling so I signalled to the bench and John brought on Micky Gynn.

65 minutes: MIKE LIGGINS: I have to say, Stuart, we've played about 20 minutes of the second half and I just can't see where a goal is coming from for Coventry City. They haven't had any chances at all this half but there's a long way to go, I still have faith.

68 minutes: STUART LINNELL: There's Brendan Ormsby, who's defended so well for Leeds, Phillips forward there for Bennett, Ormsby in the way again...and Bennett keeps it in play, he does well Dave Bennett, plays it across the goal, McGrath can't turn it in but Michael Gynn can, YES! MICHAEL GYNN HAS SCORED FOR COVENTRY CITY! Coventry City live again in this FA Cup semi-final. Dave Bennett did so well, just as it looked as if

Brendan Ormsby was going to save the day for Leeds yet again. Houchen and Borrows go to congratulate Bennett, so does Cyrille Regis, he did so well, laid the ball across goal, McGrath missed it but Michael Gynn, the substitute, closing in at the far post slotted home and it's 1-1!

MIKE LIGGINS: Match-winner Michael Gynn, lovely goal, it wasn't brilliant by any means but it's lifted Coventry City's hopes. It was Dave Bennett who won the ball off Brendan Ormsby when the ball looked to be going out of play, crossed it, Lloyd McGrath missed it and, oh my goodness, I thought that was it, the end of the world had come, but then Michael Gynn hit it, the ball actually bobbled, hit the ground, and I thought he'd missed it as well but the ball went into the back of the net – RAPTURE!

JOHN SILLETT: Dave Bennett chased down Brendan Ormsby then hooked his right foot around the ball to keep it in play and dispossess him on the byline. Dave did a great job there, he didn't give it up, and there was Gynny's quick feet – BANG! I knew once we got that goal we would be safe and sound because we were good defenders. I turned to George Dalton and said, 'If that doesn't pick those boys up, nothing will, that is what our doctor prescribed.' It got the fans going and the roar when Dave dispossessed Ormsby lifted the roof off the Kop, it was full to capacity and a sea of blue and white.

DAVE BENNETT: We never gave in, we always had a go, and that moment summed up the season. I chased the ball down and always thought I could get to it purely just to keep it in play but also keep it under control and it worked to a tee but what I didn't know was that I was passing it to Lloyd who was the furthest man forward! Once I'd got off the floor I could see him right in front of goal but, no disrespect to him, thank god he missed the ball and Micky Gynn put it in!

MICHAEL GYNN: Fortunately, I made a difference. The noise at the Kop was incredible. When I scored I remember Cyrille hugged me so tight I thought he was going to break my ribs! He'd had a couple of earlier chances and the relief all around was palpable. It was an amazing noise when I scored, the most important goal of my career, without question.

NICK PICKERING: Within five or six minutes of going on he's scored!

CYRILLE REGIS: That was a turning point, it got us back level. Lloyd missed the cross and Gynny scored – I've never given Gynny a bigger hug in my life. That's the beauty of 'team', I admire people who play a one-person sport but, team sport, Micky Gynn pulled us out and we had that team ethic. It gave us a surge of energy.

LLOYD McGRATH: I came steaming into the box and missed the ball, a good job as well as it would have probably gone over the bar or the stand! I always say Micky Gynn said 'Over!' to me so that's why I left it!

GRAHAM RODGER: I was in the squad, in or around the dugout area. It was a very tense occasion but when you look at that cup run you had your big-time players produce the big-time moments when you needed them. Dave Bennett's tackle to take the ball off Brendan Ormsby, most players would have given that up. You can talk about the final but 'Benno' was absolutely magnificent in the semi-final, he was unplayable. Dave was a good player anyway but also a big-time player for the big occasion and boy did he produce when we needed him to. I got on well with 'Benno', I remember him saying to me, one time, he was always well attired, that if you look smart you play smart – that was his ethos.

STEVE OGRIZOVIC: Micky Gynn eventually levelled from Dave Bennett's pull-back. Dave was outstanding on the day and had a great cup run. Micky was a very underrated player and he drew us level, we needed to score then as the game had moved on and you begin to think, 'Is it going to be our day?' For Gynny to put the chance away was great and it put us right back in the game.

MICKY ADAMS: The game-changer was the equaliser. Brendan Ormsby, if he had his time again, would have thumped it into the stand but he tried to shepherd it out of play and 'Benno' dispossessed him and got Coventry back into the game.

TREVOR PEAKE: It was Benno that persevered and kept the ball in and thankfully Lloyd missed his shot (when you speak to him he'll hopefully say the same!). The timing of that was key, we needed Micky Gynn's goal to go in when it did because we weren't on our game.

BRIAN KILCLINE: It was the hardest game we had to play and was such a relief when we got back into the game.

The amount of fans in the Kop that day, I didn't realise there was that many people living in Coventry!

DAVID PHILLIPS: It only needed something to turn and, Brendan Ormsby, he tried to shield the ball out and all of a sudden we're level. There was a visible roar as Dave dispossessed him and crossed the ball, it missed Lloyd and fortunately fell to the right person to level. That was a huge turning point and a lesson to be learnt.

GAVIN CLIFTON: Then an amazing thing happened, Benno produced a moment of sheer magic to rob Brendan Ormsby and laid it back to Lloyd who had an air shot only to leave it for Gynn to slam it home, the Kop went mad! I'll love Dave Bennett forever for that!

MATT PARTRIDGE: We came out in the second half and were a little better until we brought on Micky Gynn. Benno robbed Ormsby and there was Gynn near the penalty spot to smash it in via the floor. There were fantastic scenes in the crowd.

DEAN NELSON: The ball looked lost until 'Benno' centred it and there was Gynn, who had just come on for Pickering, to knock it in. It wasn't a clean shot but it was in the net and that's what mattered.

LEE CORDEN: I've seen the Micky Gynn equaliser too many times on TV to remember the goal live but the celebration after was crazy. Scary. My sister disappeared under a surge of supporters and our delight turned to fear as she stayed down for what was only a matter of seconds but felt like an age. A few other fans realised what had happened and helped my dad pull her to her feet. Amazingly, there was no damage done.

ROB SUMMERFIELD: Micky Gynn had tremendous pace and a low centre of gravity. Straight away he was running at Leeds, causing panic.

77 minutes: MIKE LIGGINS: Here's a chance for Michael Gynn on the edge of the box...and it falls to Keith Houchen, he's got a chance, goes round the goalkeeper...IT'S IN! HOUCHEN SCORES! It's Coventry City 2 Leeds United 1. It was Michael Gynn on the edge of the box that created the chance, it came to Houchen, he went forward, rounded the goalkeeper and slotted it in! And Coventry City are on their way to Wembley!

STUART LINNELL: And it's the FA Cup hero, the man that always seems to rise to the occasion, I think he's shedding a little tear right now, he is the man who seems to have his name on a cup winner's medal or at least a Wembley appearance. Keith Houchen has scored Coventry City's second goal which changes the complexion of this match.

KEITH HOUCHEN: As a striker you're always looking for a chance. It was an end-to-end game, not tight by any means, and we probably should have been two or three up anyway. It's all split-second, when the ball came through to me from Micky Gynn, it's a game of reactions and

Calvin Urquhart (front) leads out the Sky Blues for the third round tie with Bolton

Terry Gibson celebrates in the fourth round tie at Old Trafford but the goal was disallowed

David Phillips tackles Stoke's Lee Dixon in the fifth round tie at the Victoria Ground – the referee waved play on

Steve Ogrizovic and Brian Kilcline celebrate with match-winner Michael Gynn after the 1-0 win at Stoke

Keith Houchen and Steve Sedgley celebrate at Hillsborough – City lead 2-1 in the quarter-final

Steve Cockrill, Lloyd McGrath, John Sillett and George Dalton as City take a 2-1 lead in the quarter-final

15,000 celebrate the 3-1 win at Sheffield Wednesday in the quarter-final

Dressing room celebrations after the extra-time win over Leeds United at Hillsborough

Recording 'Go For It City' in the front room of Steve and Heather Taylor's house

The Sky Blues appear on Blue Peter

Live on Central TV the night prior to the final at the Compleat Angler hotel, Marlow

The visit to Wembley the week before the final

Lee Corden and family all set for Wembley at Coventry station

Rob Summerfield and friends outside Wembley – dressed in black of course....

The Duchess of Kent meets the Sky Blues players prior to kick-off

Regis..
Downs..
Houchen..
Bennett..
DAVID BENNETT 1-1!

Trevor Peake and Clive Allen epitomise the spirit of the '87 final

Regis..
Houchen..
Bennett..
Houchen! Brilliant goal!

The final whistle blows at Wembley

'...and the Sky Blues are sky high...'

Dean Nelson amongst the Sky Blue Army at Wembley

Corporation Street, Coventry at the final whistle

Graham Hover's view from the bus the day after the final as the Sky Blue Army welcome their heroes

New Union Street, Coventry, Sunday 17 May 1987

Coventry Evening Telegraph

City Final

PURE MAGIC ALL THE WAY

INSIDE

YOUR SUPER CUP FINAL EIGHT-PAGE SPECIAL

It's bliss for joyful fans

SALUTING the HEROES

KEEP IN THE SWIM AT DAVIES

CANNES or COVENTRY

Coventry Evening Telegraph – Monday 18 May 1987

incidents, it was instinct and I was in. I drew Mervyn Day, I used to like rounding the keeper to score and did it often. You don't see it very often nowadays, it's a dying art and I committed Merv, an old team-mate of mine from Orient. I was used to beating him as I used to beat him in training every day! The one thing that does come into your mind, as a striker, when you round the keeper, nine times out of ten it pushes you wide and you're concentrating on hitting the target. I think Micky Adams nearly stopped it on the line but as soon as it left my foot I knew it was in but I could see them scrambling across to try and clear it off the line.

MICHAEL GYNN: I got involved on the edge of the box and nicked it through to Keith just as Brendan Ormsby swung his boot at me and his studs caught the inside of my leg, half a centimetre closer and it would have seriously injured me and I might have missed Wembley. If you see the celebrations after Keith's goal I was on the floor and my leg was killing me. I hobbled off briefly but in those days you just got on with it and we were 13 minutes from an FA Cup Final.

CYRILLE REGIS: Micky Gynn's goal gave us a surge of energy but it still wasn't over. Keith Houchen, who had been absolutely fantastic, comes in again with a goal. He couldn't score in the league but, put him in a cup game, and he was a man possessed.

STEVE OGRIZOVIC: When Keith scored to make it 2-1 everybody thought we'd done it. I hadn't had a lot to do in the second half.

DAVID PHILLIPS: At 2-1 you think everything is ok and, all of a sudden, the goal goes in but it was a question of 'never say die' instilled in us by George and John in 1986/87. We had such great camaraderie among us. We fought for each other. There were no prima donnas, just a squad of 15 who worked hard for each other. We went out drinking with each other and just carried on going.

ROB GURNEY: The goal that brought the emotion to the surface for me wasn't the winning goal as we were all so exhausted by then because of the see-sawing events unfolding on the field. I still listen back to the Mercia Sound cassette from the day and, even now, it gets me every time, when Houchen made it 2-1. I literally thought, at that moment, we were going to Wembley for the first time ever. The game was the last occasion I spent with my dad at the football as we lost touch after my parents divorced and he passed away last year. It is quite poignant for me in many ways and I can still hear 'Liggo' saying 'Houchen scores!' Those words bring it all back.

IAN WOODS: I remember describing Houchen's shot had been sucked into the net by the Coventry fans behind the goal. I went down to the tunnel area around the 80-minute mark not thinking it would go into extra time, ready to do the post-match interviews. When Leeds levelled shortly afterwards to take the tie into extra time I decided it wasn't worth going back up to sit in the stand with Kirk, it had been a hassle getting down to the tunnel area with the usual jobsworths around so I stood in the tunnel and watched the match from there. At one point 'Liggo' handed over to me for a word with Kirk but got me describing what was happening in the respective dugouts.

MATT PARTRIDGE: The scenes for Micky Gynn's goal were reciprocated tenfold when Houchen did his Zico impression. He rounded Mervyn Day and put us in front, mayhem ensued on the Kop!

83 minutes: STUART LINNELL: We have one heck of a cup tie here now. Leeds, who had it all their way for so long in this match, now trailing, their fans quieter now and it's the City faithful in the ascendency in the vocal stakes as Leeds come again though.

Brian Kilcline wins that one in the air, Downs with the tackle against Ritchie, Michael Gynn comes in to help out...Ritchie keeps possession though and sends it across the area and THERE IT IS, THEY'RE BACK ON TERMS! Keith Edwards has scored for Leeds United with a header when it looked as if Coventry had cleared the danger and the Coventry City defence just can't believe it.

MIKE LIGGINS: Oh well, back to the drawing board, still time. Keith Houchen, he can't believe it, saying to his defenders 'How could you do it to me,' 2-2 the score and have we got a cup tie.

STEVE OGRIZOVIC: Keith Edwards was a goalscorer. It was the first time we'd left him free in the brief time he'd been on the pitch.

MICKY ADAMS: Keith Edwards, a proper goalscorer, levelled for us late on from Andy Ritchie's persistence out on the right wing, to take the tie into extra time.

BRIAN KILCLINE: The littlest guy on the pitch scores a bloody header!

90 minutes – Coventry City 2 Leeds United 2

BRIAN BORROWS: We didn't get going for 20 plus minutes and then our equaliser came from nowhere. We then grew into the game and were stronger. At the end of 90 minutes we had the extra-time period and Ian Baird, Leeds' centre-forward, came up and shook my hand and said, 'See you next week.' I replied, 'Next week? We've got extra time!' and he just sunk. 'You're joking?' he commented. Straightaway that gave me a spring, thinking, 'He's out on his legs here.' We had some fit players who could run all day. Dave Phillips, Nick Pickering, Lloyd McGrath, there was plenty of energy in the engine room.

JOHN SILLETT: When referee Roger Milford blew the whistle to signal extra time I spoke to the lads on the pitch and told them, in front of us, we've got the greatest opportunity you will ever have as players to get to the one place which I think is the king of kings in football – Wembley. I said you are the fitter side, you play the better football, you've got to accept that it's your responsibility to carry this club into somewhere they have never been before. The boys took to it and we gave everyone a swig of whisky – we had Lloyd McGrath, who was the quietest lad I ever had to deal with as a professional footballer, and he started singing again, after his half-time rendition, 'Here we go, here we go...' and everybody picked it up. Even the

Leeds boys were looking across the pitch at us, thinking, 'What's going on here?'

99 minutes: MIKE LIGGINS: Michael Gynn with the free kick on the Coventry right, it's almost on the Leeds byline, just outside the box. He's got Regis, Kilcline and Houchen waiting, he floats it in now, up goes Regis, nods down, Houchen's in there... BENNETT – GOAL! Coventry 3 Leeds 2, the free kick taken by Michael Gynn, Cyrille Regis headed it down, Keith Houchen had a poke and there was Dave Bennett to hit it home, another one of the Coventry match-winners, and might, might we be on the way to Wembley?

DAVE BENNETT: Someone once asked me had I ever played the perfect game. I'd have to say it was this game, you have a hand in the goal to get us back into the game, a contribution to Keith's and then going on to score the winner. Everything goes for you. I was having a battle with Micky Adams and then all of a sudden the game has changed in more ways than one.

MATT PARTRIDGE: When 'Benno' put us into the lead again I opened my mouth and nothing came out, pure silence, I was all roared out!

BLAKE WAUGH: Leeds gave us a great game but you just sensed we were going to win and we were on our way to Wembley!

JOHN POYNTON: I was sat with FA chairman Sir Bert Millichip at Hillsborough. When we scored the winner I jumped up to celebrate and when I sat back down he said, 'You mustn't do that in the cup final, it's not the done thing to do.' The atmosphere that day was fantastic.

120 minutes: MIKE LIGGINS: And the Coventry City fans are on their feet, the whole stand, they're stamping their feet, waving their scarves, the sun's shining down on them.

STUART LINNELL: I make it that time is up, we're playing time added on at the end of extra time. Throw-in to be taken by Greg Downs who will take his time, takes it to Michael Gynn, Gynn keeps possession, goes on a little trot across the park, lays it across to Dave Bennett and THERE IS THE FINAL WHISTLE! COVENTRY CITY WILL PLAY AT WEMBLEY ON 16 MAY AGAINST TOTTENHAM HOTSPUR IN THE FINAL OF THE FA CUP!

NEVILLE FOULGER: In a sense, Coventry were fortunate they were going to play on the same ground as in the quarter-final and then being housed in the Kop end. The semi-final was fantastic. I can always remember the sight of the Sky Blue scarves, a sea of Sky Blue and white. It was a nail-biter and it was almost because of the 3-2 scoreline that I predicted they would win the final by the same score.

A lot of the on-field events left you gasping. It was a memorable game but, again, lady luck, in a way, went Coventry's way for the first time. Little moments in the game, like Bennett dispossessing Ormsby, to come through it 3-2 was sensational. For me there was no real particular moment that stands out. It was just the whole thing. All the way through you wouldn't have wanted to predict a winner, you just had this feeling, 'This has to be our year.' Everything was falling into place and the feeling at the final whistle was just unbelievable. It was that moment the realisation dawned for the first time in 104 years that we were going to Wembley. I've been to the stadium many times to cover England matches and cup finals so going there wasn't that big for me but it was massive to be able to report on Coventry City playing there. The scenes on the pitch afterwards, with John Sillett, George Curtis and the fans were just sensational.

STEVE SEDGLEY: I was on the bench again but never got on. As the final whistle blew I hugged John Sillett and all the lads were giving me stick later on, they said I was only hugging him so I would get a spot in the team at Wembley! I was itching to get on. It was a nerve-wracking game, but because it was so tight I don't think John wanted to change things after he'd sent on Micky Gynn in place of Nick when he got injured. I can understand that, putting an 18-year-old kid on in such circumstances, it could have backfired on him, and we got the right result.

JOHN SILLETT: Winning the semi-final was possibly the greatest moment – getting to Wembley. It was everybody's dream in football. I thought, 'At least we've achieved something never done before in the history of the club.' It was a superb atmosphere and we played some beautiful football. I was a believer in football, my biggest change at Coventry was changing the style of football. I always thought we used Cyrille the wrong way, his lungs weren't the greatest to have to chase all the long balls into the channels but on sprints he was fantastic, ten to 12 yards, tremendous pace and power. We had to play down the sides of the centre-halves to Cyrille and he would get on the end of it. I had a meeting with the boys when I first took over and said, 'How do you want to play?' I said, 'Your way or my way?' to which they replied, 'What's your way?' and I responded, 'Winning!'

Giving the ball away, you were the opposition's best player. They never had to win it, you gave it to them. They achieved this new style with great distinction. We were a good side to watch purely from changing the system. I worked a lot on the back four. I always thought we had good players. Greg was a good player who could pass the ball, he was shrewd and knew the game. Trevor Peake, to this day, was the best reader of the game I ever dealt with.

Kilcline was honest, a wonderful captain, did a brilliant job on the field and was a great striker of a football. He was powerful and opposition players were frightened of him. I thought we had the best right-back in the country, Brian Borrows, he was the unluckiest player never to play for England. We weren't to get wider than the 18-yard box which meant the wide men had to cover the gap between the box and the touchline and 'Benno' and Pickering did this beautifully. 'Benno' worked so hard, he did a great job tracking back and had a great engine. On his day he was unstoppable and thank god Wembley was the day but he had many good days. Nick Pickering was very honest, a good player with a great engine in front of Greg and it worked a treat.

GREG DOWNS: On the coach back to Coventry I said to John, 'I've had a nightmare today.' He replied, 'We all have them but we're a team and we'll get through it together.' We were all mates which is why we all get together still, we weren't just a football club, we enjoyed each other's company off the pitch, where, as entertainments manager, that was my domain and I used to call the nights out. I think too much is sometimes made of the 'team spirit'. We didn't win the cup on team spirit, we won it on ability; the team spirit always helped us stick together when things weren't going our way.

NICK PICKERING: In that second half, the last 20 minutes we came through and for your club to get to Wembley for the first time is fantastic. It's a massive game with such a lot of pressure but, in the end, we won easily in extra time. I'm watching all this with a dead leg, you think you've won it at 2-1 and then Keith Edwards, a goalscoring machine came on, to level, a little loss of concentration by us. We could have won by four or five in the second half of extra-time, they played really well. The fans were fantastic, it was a massive rollercoaster and I've got wonderful memories of it all.

MICKY ADAMS: At the end of the game John Sillett and George Curtis came into the Leeds dressing room to wish me well which was a nice touch and appreciated.

STEVE OGRIZOVIC: The atmosphere at Wembley was great but, because the whole arena is just away from the pitch there was something about the atmosphere in the semi-final. The noise from the Kop cascaded down on to the pitch and stayed there. It literally was the best atmosphere I've experienced at a football match I played in. Hillsborough's Kop was packed to the rafters and our fans were absolutely brilliant.

It was probably better than Wembley that day because the fans were so close to the action, it was impossible to make yourself heard, absolutely terrific.

To win in those circumstances and to see the fans going delirious, as a group of players we probably realised what we'd achieved in reaching Wembley. It was everybody in Coventry's wish and we fulfilled it, we saw that with the homecoming after the game as people were on the bridges as we entered Coventry. It was just a carnival atmosphere with everybody enjoying themselves. We were very fortunate as players to be the ones to do that.

BRIAN BORROWS: It was a fantastic achievement to reach the final. Forget about winning it at that stage, just thinking that the team had got to Wembley was just unbelievable. Both games at Hillsborough had great atmospheres.

CYRILLE REGIS: Everybody's legs were hanging off by the final whistle but the 'team' carried us through to Wembley.

DEAN EMERSON: It seemed a repeat of the Wednesday game, two goals in quick succession and there was a confidence in the team after the United tie that we weren't going to lose in the cup. It was a squad of players who all gelled together.

STEVE LEE: It wasn't an easy game at all, it went to extra time and I remember it being really hard work for Coventry. After the game George Curtis wouldn't let any media through except the locals – Bob Hall, myself, local radio and photographers. We interviewed the players in the dressing room for a piece on Monday evening's *Midlands Today* show.

IAN BOLTON: After the game I'd done some interviews with players on the pitch as they celebrated victory and then I went to the dressing room area. The door to the Coventry changing room was shut with quite a crowd gathered. George Curtis was 'on the door' which opened about six inches and there was George's face – he just said, 'You, you and you.' Fortunately, he recognised me from the earlier rounds with Mercia and in I went!

IAN WOODS: At the final whistle Stuart handed over to me pretty quickly and I made my way on to the pitch. My abiding memory at the final whistle was the wall of Sky Blue at the Kop end erupting in celebration. I was completely overwhelmed by the sight of all the Sky Blues fans, it was such an impressive Kop and with all the scarves and flags it was really special. I took over the commentary to describe the scenes on the pitch and then went into the Coventry dressing room for more interviews with the players. All this time I was still wearing the lucky yellow jumper. I spoke with Trevor Peake, Houch and 'Killer'. Looking back now it's extraordinary we did the interviews out on the pitch, rounded up what happened, interviewed again in the dressing room and were off air shortly after the final whistle. No phone-ins, no post-match analysis, a completely different world now!

MATT KERR: We were in the stand for the game, right next to the Leeds fans. I'd never heard such noise at a game from opposition fans, they were banging on the hoardings and my granddad commented in his Welsh accent that they were as loud as the war! There was such togetherness throughout the cup run with great memories still so clear to this day.

MATT PARTRIDGE: I came back on the Coventry special with a contented smile on my face knowing I was off to Wembley with my beloved City!

GAVIN CLIFTON: In what would become a dress rehearsal for what was to come in the final 'Benno' found a finish and, after what seemed like an age, we were there! What a game! What a day! It was capped off, back in the pub later on in the evening, seeing Billy sat there clutching a pint of milk and still in his slippers!

KEV MONKS: The Sky Blues were on their way to Wembley! We walked through the Leeds fans who were talking about how they were happy to be alive after a scary time on the Leppings Lane terrace and shook hands with England World Cup winner Nobby Stiles whose son John played in the Leeds midfield. It took an age to get out of Sheffield and when we got back to Coventry, which was before the coaches, we drove down the Ansty Road and saw people out with flags and scarves. I walked into the Rose and Crown that night and the place was in uproar when some of the City team walked in. That pub was a regular hangout for the players during the FA Cup run and the likes of Cyrille Regis and Dave Bennett were carried shoulder high round the pub. I can't remember getting home but it was light by the time I did get in and still on a massive high.

ROB SUMMERFIELD: When Dave Bennett scored what proved to be the winner there was a feeling of release like no other. Pouring out of the ground that day remains my best ever moment in football. We were in the cup final, the dream had come true.

LEE CORDEN: The celebrations at the end were like nothing I'd ever experienced and my dad maintains, to this day, that the semi-final was, in many ways, a sweeter feeling than the final itself.

MOZ BAKER: I was on the Kop against Leeds but so nearly didn't make the game. I'd had, way in advance, my engagement party booked for Saturday 11 April and this caused a bit of an issue because my girlfriend said I couldn't possibly go as I wouldn't be back in time. This was a huge problem for me but then it was changed to the Sunday which was such a relief! It was the one game we were expected to win, Bolton aside, and typical Coventry City it was about to go pear-shaped. When the game turned in the 69th minute I just felt we were going to win from that point onwards. The atmosphere was incredible, the crowd were great that day and the Kop was a real pleasure to be stood on, it was magical. It was a really special day, that end of the ground contained the noise really well under the roof and there was a real sense of achievement. The fans drove the team on and the football club was as one.

NEIL WHITE: We walked away from the ground with thousands of dumbstruck City fans. The celebrations were incredibly muted because we couldn't comprehend what the team had just done.

IAN WOODS: I watched the highlights on the TV later that night and they showed some features in the dressing room area where I could see myself conducting interviews with all concerned. I've still got it on video somewhere.

JIM BROWN: Unfortunately, I had to miss the semi-final. I'd won a family holiday through work and a week-long trip to Madeira beckoned. I couldn't believe my bad luck. Not only were there no mobile phones or internet in those days but the cost of a call to the UK was prohibitive. I finally managed to speak to a friend about three hours after the final whistle to discover we had reached Wembley.

DEAN NELSON: The ref blew his whistle and we were there at long last, tears rolling down the cheeks of young and old and thoughts of people no longer here. Sunday 12 April 1987 the day we reached Wembley. OMG now to get a Wembley ticket!

BOB EALES: I was still at sea and the duty officer on the day, stuck on the ship with nowhere to go. Unfortunately, the quartermaster for the day was a Leeds fan so I was kept up-to-date with the score until later on when he failed to tell me the final score. Once I found out he got it both barrels!

ANDY SCAYSBROOK: I will never forget that day, it was the greatest as a City fan so far. The game and the reception we got that night when the travelling army of City fans were welcomed home by fans who couldn't make the game waving from bridges and the side of the road as we made our way back into Coventry. It brought a lump to my throat and it was my first real experience of what a united City could do united by football. Little did we know at that time what the night of Saturday May 16 1987 would herald for the citizens of Coventry.

GEOFF FOSTER: I don't know what was more of a shock, the Sky Blues getting to Wembley or our bus making it to South Yorkshire and back! One other memory of the day was the Lord Mayor of Coventry, Winnie Lakin, before the kick-off, walking in front of the Kop to thank the thousands of Sky Blues fans for their support.

The other semi-final, at Villa Park, saw Tottenham beat Watford 4-1 to book their place in the Wembley showpiece. Watford, hamstrung by goalkeeping injuries, were 3-0 down after 35 minutes to end the game as a contest.

Coventry Evening Telegraph, Monday 13 April 1987

THANKS LADS!

Victory salutes in burst of Cup fever

Cup final fever today gripped Coventry as the city prepared to march to Wembley. The Sky Blues' historic victory over Leeds United at Hillsborough yesterday has sparked off city-wide celebration. And it looks set to carry on right the way up to the final in London on 16 May. Factory workers clocked on today still wearing their Sky Blue caps and scarves while shopfloors were buzzing with excited talk about the prospect of City's first FA Cup Final in 104 years.

The atmosphere at the Coventry City Supporters Club last night and today was jubilant. Chairman Jim Hamill, a supporter for 50 years, said, 'It's just fantastic. It's something I thought I would never see in my lifetime. It has got everybody buzzing.' Former chairman Jimmy Hill joined the chorus of praise. He said, 'It was one of the best semi-finals I can ever remember, a splendid game of football.'

The Sky Blues were 3-1 to win the FA Cup after 90 minutes with rivals Spurs 6-5 ON. If the game stretched to extra time, you could get 7-4 City, 4-9 the Londoners.

Sillett's role of honour

Curtis: He's the man in charge of the team – the only man to lead us out at Wembley

John Sillett will become the first coach to lead a team out in an FA Cup final at Wembley. Coventry City managing director George Curtis confirmed that it will be Sillett at the head of the Sky Blues players when they walk down the Wembley tunnel alongside Tottenham Hotspur on Saturday 16 May.

FA rules decree that only one man is allowed to lead out the team at soccer's most glamorous occasion. It has always been the manager, but though Curtis 'outranks' his former playing colleague in their unique managerial partnership, he has decided to step aside at Wembley.

Sillett, 'It will be the greatest thrill of my life to walk out with the lads at Wembley. It is a fairy-tale and I don't think I'll ever come back to earth.'

Curtis, 'There's only one man to lead the team out at Wembley and that's John. There's never been any question about that. This is a marvellous day for the club and I'm not interested in comparing it to those great days of the 1960s. You can't live in the past. It's just very pleasing for John and myself and particularly all the players who were written off as a bunch of has-beens at the start of the season. We may not have a side packed with star names like some clubs, just a team willing to give everything for the club. The character and spirit is unbelievable.'

JOHN SILLETT: George used to book the hotels, coach and the like. He booked the Hilton at the top of Wembley Way so I said to him we'd better go and look at it. I had the biggest moaners in the squad if the hotel wasn't right – Steve Ogrizovic would moan about his bed, the food so I told George we had to get it right. We drove to Wembley and the manager of the Hilton took me to where our rooms were, all down one side of the corridor. I asked him who was on the other side of the corridor, he replied, 'The press,' to which I replied, 'I'm sorry, we're not going to stay here,' so then we had to drive back and went through Marlow where I had heard there was a good hotel. We looked and found it, The Compleat Angler.

Coventry Evening Telegraph, Tuesday 14 April 1987

City unveil tickets plan

Coventry City fans will have to become season ticket holders or Executive Club members to make sure of a place at Wembley. There will be a chance for other fans to snap up any remaining tickets on Sunday 10 May on a first come, first served basis. Even then they will need to produce FIVE ticket stubs taking in the semi-final and the four remaining home games. All current season ticket holders, fully paid up Executive Club members, pools agents and club shareholders are each guaranteed one ticket for Wembley. Prices and selling details will be announced as soon as possible. Remaining tickets from the 25,000 cup final allocation – there are expected to be about 15,000 – will then become available to those buying a season ticket, joining the Executive Club or producing five stubs.

Season ticket prices were as follows: Terrace £68.50, Terrace seats £87, West Stand £98.50, Sky Blue Stand £107 and £127, Main Stand £127 and £147.

GRAHAM HOVER: No one should ever forget how special a year it was for Coventry, it was a great year. I missed only three or four games away from home in all my years at the club. Cup football, certainly in those days, was fantastic. Everyone used to get excited by it, it hasn't got the same meaning now because of the way it is treated by certain managers which is a shame, but in that era it was something special. Things change, sometimes for the worse, and finance dictates so much nowadays as TV pays clubs so much money. In those days it was great to get up on a Saturday morning and to be able to sit there with the whole family in front of the TV for the whole day – it was an event as there was so little live football available at that time.

In 1987 we didn't have a lot of staff at the club, that was the biggest thing, there was no call for large numbers of staff. In the office there was myself, my wife who was my secretary, we had a receptionist, two or three in the ticket office where Bernard was the full-time manager and he had a couple of part-timers with him. It was nigh on impossible to cope with the demands for tickets especially as we got nearer to Wembley. How we coped I'll never know, we got people in to help but there was a lot of criticism and you can't satisfy everyone. We had to make some brave decisions.

It was an enjoyable time, but hard work, because it was something special and everyone was buzzing about just how good everything was. It was a pleasure to work in such an environment. The systems were not computerised in 1987, we had the tickets printed for us and then we had to check them all individually. For the final itself, we had 25,000 tickets sent to us by the FA and we had to check every single one. I remember bringing them home and we had friends staying with us that weekend. The four of us spent the whole time counting the tickets, checking every single one. It was incredible.

The tickets were under our bed as I had to put them somewhere safe! After that, to issue them to supporters (the FA two years prior had determined they wanted to know everyone who had a ticket to ensure no touts could get hold of any) we had to log every ticket manually, a complete paper trail.

The players had something like six tickets, I think, and rightly so because they got us to Wembley. Before the cup year we were averaging 10,000 or 11,000 at Highfield Road, 25,000 should have been more than adequate but, of course, it never works that way.

STEVE & HEATHER TAYLOR: After a nail-biting semi-final the reality suddenly hit us. We had just one full day to prepare for what was to date the most pressure and pleasure anyone could wish for. We were going to entertain the whole of the FA Cup final team at our house! Who wouldn't want that?

We gained a bit of financial support in the shape of a loan from Granada Bingo who were sponsoring the club at the time. The money was handed over at the old Coventry theatre which had become a bingo hall. The manager collected from various areas of the club, including the slot machines, £2,500 in cash (pennies etc all in money bags) to pay for the vinyl pressings! We agreed to do the recording and production in exchange for a cup final ticket!

Tuesday 14 April arrived, it was a beautiful sunny day and far too hot to record a hit single. We were up early and had hired some extra equipment from Birmingham. John, the guy we hired it from, insisted on staying to help. The team arrived separately, gradually accumulating outside our house, and were playing the radio commentary of the semi-final on one of their cars' cassette players. Their cars, along with the media, were parked up the entire length of our road. It really was bizarre and could never happen today!

Joe Stainer, the agent employed by the club, sent some cans of lager round while we also provided some. It set the scene for an amazing day ahead!

John Sillett had sent the team round on their own. He tried to find the 'studio' but no one he asked for directions knew where it was so he never made it. The backing track was already done so all that was left to do was add the team vocal. They had never heard *Go For It* City before but right from the Greg Downs count-in they took to it really well in the makeshift studio which was, of course, our lounge. David Phillips remarked that he'd sang the first verse into the chandelier! In reality, the microphones were wired to the upstairs bedroom studio where John was pressing 'stop' and 'start' on the Tascam 8 track recorder!

It would have been a lot easier if the TV, radio and press hadn't descended on the house. The little semi-detached in Keresley was suddenly transformed into the hottest location in Britain. Although it was potential mayhem the recording went well and everyone had a ball, despite Oggy saying after the first take, 'Hey, why don't three of us sing a solo,' and the rest of the team taking the mickey! It was all amazingly good humoured and the lads actually sang really well and gave it all they'd got. During a break they sat on the front lawn and the girl delivering the local paper must have thought that all of her Christmases had come at once! After giving interviews and drinking most of the 48 cans they left. The next-door neighbours got autographs on the way out, the least they deserved for putting up with the 'noise' all day!

STEVE OGRIZOVIC: In those days a cup final song was part and parcel of the cup run, everybody did one. When we were asked to go to the studios to record the song we expected some top recording studio but ended up going to their house in Keresley to their front room! Back then you played hard and enjoyed yourself off the pitch. All of our cars lined the road, we'd all travelled there individually, it would never happen nowadays!

BRIAN KILCLINE: Just where did all that beer come from? But it all went!

Coventry Evening Telegraph, Wednesday 15 April 1987

Curtis: Preparations must be right

City 'no' to cash offers

Managing director George Curtis today cut through all the Wembley hype to insist, 'We are going there to win the FA Cup – not make up the numbers.' And as cash offers for promotional activities on the big day poured in, the Coventry City supremo made it clear the Sky Blues won't be pushed into any change of routine.

They have already turned down around £50,000 by rejecting lucrative offers to change their strip, change their coach company and permit television cameras on their coach on the journey from the hotel to Wembley.

A new shirt deal would have brought in £25,000 but Curtis said, 'We don't need a new look strip because we make our own at the Big T company based at Walsall. We'll have a special strip for the day with a Wembley logo on it.' City have also turned down an £18,000 offer from a coach company who wanted to provide their transport on 16 May.

Six days after the Hillsborough triumph City travelled to Kenilworth Road, Luton, to begin a run of eight league games in 21 days prior to Wembley. The Hatters won 2-0 in a fixture that saw youth team striker Steve Livingstone make his debut as a replacement for Greg Downs.

Two days later the Mexican wave appeared at Highfield Road for the first time as an inspired second-half performance against Queens Park Rangers saw City win 4-1 in front of just under 21,000 supporters, the crowd swelled by the ticket stub incentive towards a ticket for Wembley. David Phillips's piledriver in the closing minutes put the seal on a fine win which maintained the Sky Blues' tenth place in the First Division. Nick Pickering was still absent after his semi-final injury while Livingstone made his home debut late on in the second half.

Coventry Evening Telegraph, Thursday 23 April 1987

CITY SET FOR A WEMBLEY KNEES-UP

Sky Blues fans have been promised a cracking Wembley celebration – regardless of the result of next month's cup final showdown with Spurs. The Coventry team is to be given a hero's welcome on the outskirts of the city the day after the game and will parade in an open-topped bus through bunting-draped streets. And the City Council is planning to throw in £25,000 to help the celebrations along. Tory deputy leader Tim Sawdon said, 'The players have done well – so let's give them a good booze-up.'

The players' triumphant bus tour will end at the Council House and they will appear on the balcony of the main redbrick extension overlooking Little Park Street. The bus tour route includes Broadgate, Trinity Street and the High Street. After appearing at the Council House, the players will go to the Hotel Leofric, where a banquet for 500 will be held in their honour. The guest list will be drawn up by the football club and it will cost the council around £15 a head.

Former Sky Blue Ian Butterworth put through his own net at Carrow Road to level matters at 1-1 after Kevin Drinkell had given Norwich a first-half lead in the First Division clash. City remained in tenth place with the Wembley showpiece just three weeks away.

Mick Coop's youth team travelled to Charlton Athletic for the first leg of the FA Youth Cup Final at Selhurst Park. Craig Middleton's goal, created by twin brother Lee in the 23rd minute, gave City a lead they carried into the second half before Carl Leaburn teamed up with Ronnie Mauge for the latter to level in the 68th minute. Middleton replaced injured Steve Livingstone in the City line-up while goalkeeper Paul Bastock was presented with the man of the match award.

Defeated FA Cup semi-finalists Watford, under Graham Taylor, responded to their 4-1 thumping at Villa Park with four straight wins.

The run came to an end as City left Vicarage Road 3-2 victors thanks to Greg Downs, Keith Houchen and Lloyd McGrath.

Two days later the largest home attendance since 1981's League Cup semi-final against West Ham, 26,657 watched Nick Pickering's low finish take three points for the first time against the mighty Liverpool since Terry Gibson's hat-trick in the 4-0 triumph back in 1983. The games came thick and fast as just two days later at Filbert Street soon-to-be-relegated Leicester City clawed back a late equaliser through Paul Ramsay after Michael Gynn had put the Sky Blues into the ascendency. The point took City up to eighth position with just two league fixtures to complete before the trip to Wembley.

Coventry City Matchday Programme, Wednesday 6 May 1987

CUP FINAL TICKETS

Tickets for the above match are priced as follows:

Seats: £30.00 £25.00 £17.50 £10.00

Terrace: £6.00

Ticket application forms were issued to supporters on the turnstiles at the Liverpool fixture. Priority went to season ticket holders who purchased their ticket before 14 March 1987 and they were permitted one ticket per season ticket book, at any price, subject to availability upon production of their season ticket and ticket application form. Priority then went to season ticket holders who purchased between 14 March and 14 April 1987.

Those in the Main, Sky Blue and West Stands were allowed one ticket at any price, and those in the Main Stand Enclosure, West, Sky Blue and East Terraces were allocated one terrace ticket at £6. Those who purchased between 15 April and 25 April 1987 were allocated one terrace ticket at £6 while supporters who produced a ticket stub from home fixtures against Queens Park Rangers, Liverpool, Manchester United, Southampton along with the Leeds semi-final could apply for one terrace ticket at £6 on a first come, first served basis.

YOUR TRAIN TIMES TO THE CUP FINAL

British Rail will be running nine trains to Wembley Central for the FA Cup Final at the following times: **10:15; 10:23; 10:40; 10:50; 11:04; 11:19; 11:30; 11:40** and **11:53.**

The return fare will be **£6**.

The penultimate home game welcomed Manchester United to Highfield Road. Norman Whiteside's early goal was cancelled out late on by Michael Gynn's fine low strike in front of over 23,000 supporters. On 7 March, a week prior to the quarter-final tie, 12,846 were present for the clash with Sheffield Wednesday. Since that day the subsequent home fixtures drew crowds of 23,924 (Oxford), 20,926 (Queens Park Rangers) and 26,657 (Liverpool).

KEV MONKS: Having been asked to help out in the club shop/ticket office after the semi-final, I was the first person in Coventry to have a ticket for the final at Wembley. I bagged my ticket as soon as they arrived at the club before they went on sale to the City supporters. The day of the final drew nearer and I was selling cup final tickets to thousands of fans. In the club shop everything which had Coventry City on it was selling and the hours got longer and longer. The atmosphere was amazing and I even joined those camping out when the tickets went on general sale, staying out all night then going back to work to start selling the tickets when the office opened.

ANDY TURNER: With our place booked at Wembley the next hurdle was getting hold of a ticket. Safe in the knowledge we had the all-important stubs to qualify, my parents and Michael's dad, David, joined the queues at Highfield Road the morning they went on sale as I wandered into my first lecture of the day oblivious to the chaos unfolding 120-odd miles away. Having arrived at different times, David had managed to get ahead, eventually finding himself near the counter. The problem was, although he had the stubs firmly in his grasp, my parents had the cash and couldn't get it to him. My mum's best efforts to sweet-talk a jobsworth WPC to push through to reach him were to no avail. Just as she was about to break the line and make a run for it, my dad, a probation officer by profession, spotted a solicitor he knew from court duty who happened, as luck would have it, to be an associate director at the club and kindly offered to use his position to pass the readies to the front of the queue.

Sorted! My parents had played a blinder and it remains a huge family talking point to this day whenever we reminisce about City's finest hour. Dad and I relive Houchen's glorious diving header while mum insists on recalling every minute of the ticketing scrum. She would have walked over hot coals to get me that ticket, mind you, she's never let me forget it!

DEAN NELSON: Fans queued around Highfield Road days before they went on sale with some even building tents in the players' car park. You needed a semi-final ticket stub along with four other stubs to get a cup final ticket and I had a pocket full of stubs as I needed four tickets as we were now at the general sale stage with season ticket holders having already got theirs. Rumours were going round as to how many were left so I decided to skip work on the Monday and queue for them but then I saw my boss who said, 'What are you doing here?' to which I replied,

'Same as you!' 'Too right,' came his answer. It was slow going and we were there for hours. Eventually I got to the front and had them in my hand, four Wembley FA Cup Final tickets at £6 each, what a bargain! I travelled back to Bulkington to see my sister on the way home and then heard on Mercia Sound that all the tickets had sold out. Wow, how lucky was I! There were no mobile phones back then so my sister didn't know I'd got them. I pulled up on her driveway, went in, and she'd heard the radio report. I said they'd sold out, she said never mind. I then replied, 'After I'd got ours YESSSSSSSSSSSSSS!' We jumped around the kitchen, hugged and cried. Our mum who introduced us to the City was no longer with us as she had died 12 years earlier, aged just 43. Four of us were going on that greatest of Sky Blue days with one more watching from above.

ROB SUMMERFIELD: Slowly but surely in the weeks leading up to the final Coventry became a Sky Blue wonderland. By the week of the big game it seemed every car and house was decorated with the club's famous signature colour. I also recall the sleepovers outside Highfield Road as fans camped out over a number of nights waiting for tickets to go on sale. Those early spring nights contained an air of magic. Walking home from the pub seeing all the banners and flags it was like all your CCFC Christmases had come at once.

LEE CORDEN: It never entered my head that we might not get cup final tickets, I just took it as a given that we'd been to every round so we'd take our rightful place at Wembley. The only way to guarantee tickets was for my dad to buy us all season tickets for the 1987/88 campaign. The club were cashing in and you couldn't really blame them. My parents found the money and we were on our way to Wembley after camping out in the queue to make sure we didn't miss out. Fans with ticket stubs from so-many matches could also get tickets and I remember a temporary 'refugee' camp being set up in a car park at Highfield Road that formed a queue ahead of them going on sale. We set up camp there too in order to get hold of tickets for other members of the family. It resulted in my brother taking a day off school (he was 16) to man our tent only to find his illness story blown when he appeared on *Midlands Today* that night!

Between the semi-final and final there was a party atmosphere at Highfield Road during the league matches. The 4-1 win over QPR stands out. As the Mexican wave made its way around the ground I turned around and, sat in the West Terrace in a Coventry City shirt, was the Liverpool 'fan' from the year above at school who I refused to pay my first ever gambling debt to. Part of me was annoyed at his lack of embarrassment that he was a glory supporter and bandwagoner but, equally, I felt as smug as a nine-year-old can at being right about Coventry City all along.

MOZ BAKER: As I'd been doing my work for the blind I applied for a press pass for the final as we wanted to do a special programme but Wembley wouldn't tell me if I could get a pass or not and getting hold of a ticket had become a concern. In the end I joined the Executive Club and didn't get a press pass so I was able to get a terrace ticket for behind the goal.

NEIL WHITE: We then had to work out how to get our tickets. I'm pretty sure I had bought a season ticket by then but neither Steve nor Andi had one so we had to buy tickets for several home league matches in order for us to qualify. We couldn't even go to the games because we were on holiday for a couple of weeks in April and it was at that time my dad paid for someone to stand in the queue for two days. In return, I bought Sutton Coldfield's FA Cup ticket (all FA members were sent two) so he could go to the game too.

Coventry Evening Telegraph, Friday 8 May 1987

Sky Blues Wembley shirts to be dropped

KIT DEAL WORTH SMART £150,000

Sky-high Coventry City have signed a three-year deal believed to be worth around £150,000 with Danish kit firm Hummel. It comes into effect from 1 August and means that next Saturday's Wembley FA Cup Final will be the last time the current strip is worn by the squad. The move is bound to anger the 4,000 fans who have paid out around £13 for replicas of the blue and white striped shirt worn during the cup campaign.

Club vice-chairman Ted Stocker admits the Sky Blues were hoping to keep news of the kit change quiet until after the showpiece with Tottenham, 'It is an excellent deal. We have been offered an awful lot of money just for wearing Hummel shirts.'

Last month the club turned down a £25,000 shirt deal from Hummel to change their strip for the final. Sources inside the sportswear trade claim the shirts will be similar to those worn by Denmark, who are also supplied by Hummel. The new deal does not affect the substantial sponsorship already paid by Granada Social Clubs for their name on Coventry's shirts.

JOHN POYNTON: Wembley allowed the teams to visit the week before to get a feel for the atmosphere and see which dressing room you were in. You could train out on the pitch and this is where the build-up really started. I said to Oggy, 'I tell you what, if you want a new contract, I'm going to take three penalties against you and, providing I score all three, I'm sure we will come to a satisfactory agreement.' As such, I did actually score all three!

JOHN SILLETT: Only three of the team had played at Wembley previously; Cyrille Regis for England against Northern Ireland in 1982, Nick Pickering for Sunderland against Norwich in the 1985 Milk Cup Final and Dave Bennett for Manchester City in the replayed 1981 FA Cup Final against Tottenham. Oggy was also there as substitute keeper in 1978 for Liverpool against Bruges in the European Cup Final.

STEVE COCKRILL: The day before the Southampton game we went down to Wembley. I was just about getting my back sorted out so I trained with the first team on the pitch – that was just fantastic – I've played at Wembley!

The final day of the league season, 9 May, on the day interest rates were cut by half a per cent to nine per cent, their lowest since mid-1984, a festival atmosphere ensued at Highfield Road with just seven days until the Sky Blues would step out at Wembley. Southampton were the visitors on a gloriously sunny day, themselves in a mid-table position, while City were ninth with 14 home wins out of 20 games – a club record in the First Division. In a carnival atmosphere, spectacular strikes by Brian Kilcline and Saints' George Lawrence in front of 22,620 supporters, ensured the spoils were shared and a final placing of tenth was secured. The average crowd attendance was 16,060, at the same time 12 months earlier the figure was 11,590. All of this, however, was overshadowed by a knee injury to City right-back Brian Borrows.

BRIAN BORROWS: I'd played nearly every game and John Sillett had asked me if I wanted to have a rest prior to the final. I said no then ended up going into midfield during the game. I can recall being on the edge of their box trying to nick a ball, dangled my leg and, as it was loose, someone hit it which caused it to twist and that caused the injury. You hope it's not serious and I left the ground on crutches then had an x-ray which showed nothing.

STEVE & HEATHER TAYLOR: We had noticed that Spurs were on *Blue Peter* with their offering of 'Hot Shot Tottenham' written by Chas and Dave so I (Steve) rang the BBC and asked Lewis Bronze, the editor, if Coventry could appear on the programme. Lewis said yes and another piece of history was made on the Monday prior to the final. Again, George and John saw no reason to accompany the lads so we were left to organise the day. John Sillett had, however, told the team not to turn up too early as they would be kept hanging around. The *Blue Peter* production team were panicking by 3pm asking where the team was. They called the police, the AA and goodness knows who else to look for the coach en route and were even talking about cancelling the item!

The lads arrived just before 4pm not a bit bothered, they had been playing golf! With not much time for rehearsal, and with the actual live transmission just an hour after they had arrived, preparation for an iconic national TV show was at an absolute minimum! As it went out they lip synched to the record and the names were not quite in the right places! But, it achieved the right effect and all watching Sky Blues fans were made to feel rightly proud. Heather managed to get hold of part of the *Blue Peter* set in the shape of a huge Sky Blues shield which we had to transport home on the train and still have to this day!

We got the record round to all the relevant radio stations, I (Heather) was interviewed in the *Blue Peter* garden on the day of the recording by BBC National TV news and it was on the 9pm news that night. The BBC's

Midlands Today carried the story, Steve Lee was present at the recording while Stuart Linnell and Rob Gurney from Mercia Sound were there. We got it on the *Saint and Greavsie* show along with Radio 1 and 2, the response was incredible!

JENNY POOLE: I came to the city of Coventry in 1968 and, initially, did two weeks as a temp at the club covering for Sky Blue Rose. At the end of the two weeks I was asked if I would like to return should a position arise. Shortly afterwards I became secretary to stadium manager Neil Solman who oversaw the building of the Main Stand after the fire. I was then asked if I would like to work for Noel Cantwell. He was the first manager I was secretary to and Chris Coleman, in 2010, was my last – happy days. The weeks prior to and following the 1987 FA Cup Final were the most hectic I ever experienced in my 42 years with Coventry City Football Club. There were hundreds of letters of congratulations to respond to following the semi-final, press conferences, interviews and television appearances to arrange as well as making travelling and hotel bookings for the team. Every day there were people coming and going at the training ground making preparations for the big day.

Highfield Road hosted the second leg of the FA Youth Cup Final with the tie finely balanced at 1-1 after the draw at Selhurst Park. Adults were charged £2 entry with juveniles and senior citizens at 50p. With demand high the Main Stand, Sky Blue Stand and West Terrace were open for supporters to cheer the side on. Charlton's side included Scott Minto, Darren Pitcher, Michael Bennett, Carl Leaburn and Ronnie Mauge, who all went on to have successful careers in the game. Mick Coop's men lined up with Paul Bastock in goal, a back four of Lee Middleton, John Gowens, Tony Dobson and Anthony Smith while midfield comprised Michael Cook, Robert Smith, Howard Clark and Gary Marshall. Steve Livingstone returned after missing the first leg in place of Craig Middleton and was partnered by Paul Shepstone.

Steve Livingstone's header in extra time ensured captain John Gowens lifted the trophy in front of over 12,000 supporters. Livingstone would go on to make 42 first-team appearances and score 15 times. Ten of those came in the League Cup when he famously netted four times in the 5-0 quarter-final win against Sunderland in the 1989/90 season, his first senior goals for the club, when City were eliminated in the semi-finals by Brian Clough's Nottingham Forest over two legs. Tony Dobson appeared 63 times for the Sky Blues before both were signed by Blackburn Rovers in January 1991 prior to Kenny Dalglish's arrival. Craig and Lee Middleton, Michael Cook and Howard Clark also played first-team games for City before moving on to pastures new.

STEVE LEE: In the run-up to the final we recorded 'Coventry's Cup' with the team while a stack of lager sat in the dressing room. I went away with the squad down to Ferndown, Dorset, and it was a very relaxed camp. I still recall Mike Liggins doing a ten-minute interview with John Sillett and then announcing his battery wasn't working on his call recorder so could they record it again – John Sillett's face was a picture! On the Thursday prior to the game they were allowed to drink what they wanted as footballers did in those days. They were knocking back the white wine and played a bit of golf too.

BRIAN BORROWS: The team had gone back down to Dorset while I stayed in Coventry to get intensive treatment and I had every type of help possible to get fit. On the Wednesday I was in my lounge at home when the knee suddenly felt looser. Bits of bone had chipped off when I had the initial impact and were lodged behind the knee which is why they didn't show on the x-ray. The specialist had a look the next morning and told me straightaway I had to have an operation. There was no way I was going to be fit and John Aldridge, the British Olympic team medical surgeon, operated on the Friday and I watched the game in hospital on the Saturday. I didn't want to go all that way to Wembley if I wasn't going to play and then have to wait for the operation, I just wanted it done immediately. It was fate, bad luck and just a huge shame it happened a week before the final.

GEORGE DALTON: It was a small cartilage tear, just enough for him not to be able to play. I didn't know the extent of the injury when he came off the pitch, I knew it was bad enough for him to come off but until you get a proper look you can't see what's happened, it was very unfortunate for Brian.

DAVID PHILLIPS: With Brian Borrows unfortunately out injured I found out I was playing right-back at the Dormy hotel in Ferndown, Dorset. I went to the gents and John

Sillett walked in shortly afterwards. He turned round to me and said, 'Phillo, you know what I'm going to ask you.' I replied, 'Yes, Sill, not a problem, I'll do anything on the field of play for you and the team.'

Coventry Evening Telegraph, Friday 15 May 1987

HERE WE GO! SKY BLUES ON THEIR WAY

Coventry's cup heroes are on the way to their date with destiny. And the cheers of the region are ringing in their ears. The message today from the whole of Coventry and Warwickshire was clear: Win at Wembley for us!

The Sky Blues stars began the club's momentous weekend at the Ryton Connexion where they boarded a coach for the trip to their pre-match hotel.

JENNY POOLE: The day before the game we all gathered to wave the players off from the training ground along with children from local special schools. I hadn't had time to look for my cup final outfit so as soon as everything was done I left my office and went into Coventry city centre. I couldn't find anything so I headed home very disappointed. On the bus home heading along Ball Hill, close to Highfield Road, I noticed a Sky Blue suit in the window of a boutique. I knew immediately that was the one but, unfortunately, it was past closing time!

CYRILLE REGIS: We asked if we could have a few beers the night before and Sill told us he didn't want us in pubs. Instead, we all went to the local off-licence in Marlow and went back to the hotel, sat down playing cards and watched *Cheers* with a few pints.

BOB HALL: The night before the game they stayed at the historic Compleat Angler hotel in Marlow. On the terrace overlooking the Thames I introduced ITV's *Central News* live with the whole squad. That was the moment I knew they were going to win the cup. There was such a great team spirit, camaraderie and relaxation on the eve of the club's first potential trophy that was hard to believe, a triumph of management by John Sillett and George Curtis. The joking hadn't stopped though as John Sillett sat in the middle of the group in a Hawaiian shirt, sunglasses and wig!

GARY NEWBON: In 1987 I was a presenter and controller of sport at *Central News.* I was with Jimmy Greaves, live, the night before from The Compleat Angler. There was a bit of champagne flying around, and we sat opposite the river, it was a superb, fun programme to be a part of.

STEVE LEE: On *Midlands Today* we had a live link and Jimmy Hill was there. I was in the studio for the half-hour show titled *Coventry's Cup*. The main news was that Brian Borrows' knee injury would keep him out of the final.

JOHN POYNTON: I did a presentation to all the directors and gave them all watches. Jimmy Greaves and Ian St John came across to chat. It was a lovely evening.

GRAHAM HOVER: There was a lot of fun in 1987. The players enjoyed themselves and George and John ensured there was no pressure on them at all. They were underdogs everywhere they went but we went out to enjoy ourselves and it rubbed off on the club staff too. I was on the team coach along with John Poynton, Ted Stocker, Micky French, John Reason and Derrick Richardson. I had the opportunity to work at Coventry City for 21 years in a role that I really enjoyed and not many people can say that.

STEVE COCKRILL: I went on the team coach and had my own room at the hotel which was fabulous. I'm a size six boot and Keith Houchen was given a brand new pair of Nike boots for the final. Keith said, 'Would you do me a favour and wear my boots in for me?' I said, 'No problem, what size are they?' He replied, 'Size 11.' I had to get magazines and newspapers to fill the gap and then sat in the bath with his boots on! I ended up falling asleep in the bath that night with Houchen's boots on! I've never told the tale before.

JIM BROWN: One of my great memories was the get-together of the London Supporters' Club the night before the final at a London pub. It turned out to be a clearing house for those fans, many from overseas, who needed tickets and those members who were lucky to have a spare.

NEVILLE FOULGER: I gave my score prediction the night prior to the game, 'So it all points to a cup final classic with most of the country rooting for the Sky Blues. My bet is they will be winners as well. It's City to win another thriller – this time 3-2.'

KEV MONKS: 'Don't come back without the FA Cup!' I said to George Curtis as they headed for Wembley on the team coach.

Coventry Evening Telegraph, Saturday 16 May 1987

WEMBLEY WAY!

Army of fans laps up a Sky Blue day

Wembley Way stretched between Coventry and London today. It filled the M1 as fans poured out of the city in a dazzling stream of Sky Blue support. The atmosphere among supporters was electric blue. They were in a jubilant, joyous mood for Coventry's day of days.

MIKE LIGGINS: I drove to Wembley with Ian Woods and hadn't had much sleep the night before as we were all so incredibly excited. Back in 1987 the FA Cup Final was a huge deal. It was much bigger than it is today. I was a big football fan and the FA Cup Final for kids back then growing up in the 1970s and 80s was massive. You'd spend all day in front of the TV watching the whole event. It was my first ever visit to Wembley. I've been back a few times since then and the sense of excitement was extraordinary. I was living in Leamington at the time and went for a walk in the park at some ridiculous hour having had two hours' sleep. Mercia were broadcasting from the studios on Wembley Way and we did a programme there when we arrived.

IAN WOODS: My lucky yellow jumper was worn again on the big day. My role for Mercia was to do interviews before and after the match and watch from pitchside. I was to be assisted by an 18-year-old lad who had joined Mercia as an office junior.

ROB GURNEY: My role on the day was basically lugging Ian Woods's huge radio kit around as he was reporting from behind the goal nearest the tunnel. It was the late 80s and technology wasn't as portable as it is now.

IAN WOODS: Rob was like a Mercia mascot, he was a young lad who came into the newsroom at 16 to do work experience and get the coffees in and gradually got more and more responsibility. He would later become a top radio commentator for Mercia and BBC WM. We both sat ten yards from Ian Bolton, behind the goal at the tunnel end, alongside the photographers by the 'MILO' hoarding.

STUART LINNELL: We stayed overnight in London, along with the sound engineers. I was with Tom Wadrop, the PA announcer at Highfield Road for many years and part of the Mercia team that day. The idea was that we had a Mercia radio car which Tom would drive and we would follow from the team hotel in Marlow to Wembley. We got to their hotel at breakfast time, had a brief chat with David Phillips and then Mike Liggins was thrown in the river! We then set off for the stadium and at the entrance to the hotel grounds there was a traffic island which the team coach went round…and round…and round…we found out later John Sillett had seen a magpie and that coach was not going to leave the hotel until he had seen a second one!

We travelled towards Wembley and in the front of the coach George Curtis was stood there waving at us to get out of the way, all in jest, and then we parked up at the stadium in our pre-arranged spot. As we got out the car a big, grey, Jaguar Daimler pulled up alongside us and out of that jumped Captain Mark Phillips, then married to

Princess Anne. Unfortunately, I didn't have a tape recorder with me but we had a good chat, he being a Spurs fan.

STEVE EVANS: In early 1987 I was the Coventry rugby correspondent in the winter months and then covered cricket in the summer time over at Edgbaston with Warwickshire. In the *Coventry Evening Telegraph* offices I worked alongside fellow sports writers Neville Foulger and Roger Draper. Roger drove me to Wembley and we stayed in Marlow on the Friday. The *Coventry Evening Telegraph* sports desk virtually evacuated Corporation Street en masse. We had a mobile teleprinter and telex room in a large van, this in the days prior to computers and there was a transmitter on the roof.

JOHN SILLETT: I told the boys if we saw a wedding on cup final day we'd win. I spoke to the manager of The Compleat Angler, Mr Brown, a Coventry fan, as there was a church across the river and asked if there was a wedding on 16 May. There was and I arranged for the happy couple to take a boat across to our hotel where 'Killer' took the garter off the bride and we presented them with a football and some flowers.

TREVOR PEAKE: On the morning of the game 'Killer' made a claim for the bride's garter. The look on her husband's face when he removed it, well, you wouldn't see that in this day and age! John Sillett thought it good luck to see a wedding on the day of a game and so it proved.

JOHN POYNTON: Everyone got ready and then boarded the coach for Wembley, an hour from the hotel. We then drove down Wembley Way and went in through the tunnel with the players on to the pitch. There was an official lunch on the day that I was invited to but I wanted to walk out with the players so I gave my spot to Derrick Robins who was then club president and he took his place next to the Atletico Madrid owner, Jesus Gil, a man who got rid of managers with alarming speed. We walked around on the pitch and soaked up the atmosphere.

JENNY POOLE: I got up early on cup final day and my husband, Chris, drove me to Ball Hill where we waited for the shop to open. I bought the suit and we hurried home where I pressed it, got changed and then headed for the railway station to catch the train to London. We met up with all the Coventry City staff and had VIP treatment with breakfast en route. I finally had time to relax and concentrate on the match.

DAVID PHILLIPS: I roomed with Keith Houchen. On the morning of the game we both had a full English breakfast and he actually went for a jog before we left for the stadium.

MICHAEL GYNN: The FA Cup Final is the biggest game of your life. You don't want to get there and lose. We weren't going to let the opportunity get away from us.

GRAHAM RODGER: Nobody believes me. I literally knew I was on the bench when I walked back into the changing room at around 1.30pm. Even then I still wasn't 100 per cent sure, that's John Sillett and man-management for you. I was a young player about to get some massive news and I'm pretty sure he made the decision not to tell me until then. I remember being in the hotel, earlier in the day, with *Football Focus* on and my pen picture came up as being one of the subs. I thought, 'They've made a mistake with that, they've had a guess at our subs.' I was just going for a great day out so we did the walk on the pitch and waved to family and friends. My boots were under the number 14 peg and, at the time, they comprised my right boot and Cyrille Regis's left boot. That was the team for you, if you had a problem (my own left boot had split) somebody else sorted it out for you.

I was rooming with Michael Gynn. I woke in the morning and told him I'd just seen us win the FA Cup. He burst out laughing! I told him we were going to win 3-2 and I just wish I'd backed the hunch! The FA Cup Final was the season's showpiece, it was more glamorous than winning the title even though the title was the one you wanted to win being consistent over the whole year but to win the FA Cup was THE thing at the time. You look at the way people have messed about with it down the years, it's lost that importance kicking off at 12noon and 5pm. For me it's the Saturday after the season has finished and a 3pm kick-off. It's all about the money now, back then you used to sit around the radio on a Monday lunchtime to hear the draw but that tradition has sadly been lost.

STEVE SEDGLEY: From the semi-final onwards you've got loads to do, you're doing the song, going on *Blue Peter* and lots of people are coming up to you with commercial stuff. You've got to keep yourself fit, you don't want an injury at this stage with league games to play and you need to maintain your form. It was a lot of added pressure which people don't realise, so many distractions, and it's very difficult as your thoughts are on the cup final. You've got no chance of winning the league, you're safe from relegation and have to keep your head focused. All credit to George and John because they did just that.

DEAN EMERSON: Sill took a squad of 16 to Wembley and put me in even though I couldn't play which would be unheard of nowadays. There was only two substitutes and Paul Culpin, myself and reserve keeper Jake Findlay made up the 16. We were in the stand behind the dugouts.

ANDY TURNER: We took the coach to Wembley, getting down nice and early, taking in the famous Wembley Way for the first time and mingling with Tottenham fans with their cock-sure Cockney accents. We were the underdogs and we knew it. What's more, so did they and that made the match a terrifying prospect: the thought of defeat too much to bear. How on earth could we match the class of the First Division's leading scorer Clive Allen, the dynamic 'Diamond Lights' of Hoddle and Waddle and their Argentinean legend Ossie Ardiles?

ANDY SCAYSBROOK: We caught the train on Saturday morning out of Coventry and the queue of supporters was something to behold, everyone singing and exchanging banter as they waited for one of the many specials laid on by British Rail. I will never forget the journey as it nearly ended in disaster instead of glory. As we left Coventry, with the fans on the train in full voice and many beers being consumed, we raced across the Warwickshire countryside with the carriages ringing out with the Sky Blue song. The train had started to slow and eventually stopped dead in its tracks. We all clamoured to look out of the windows to get a glimpse of what the problem might be. British Rail officials were already at the scene and were walking alongside the train with supporters eager to find out what the problem was. I can remember the looks on our faces as they told us someone had thrown wire over the electric cable and shorted the line which resulted in our standstill. My heart sank, why would someone do that and what football team did *they* support?

The officials tried desperately to get the train shunted to the next live rails, we were just sat there, the whole train praying that we didn't miss the match. After 25 anxious minutes we were finally moving again amid rousing cheers and many thanking the man upstairs for answering our prayers. We made it into Wembley station and literally ran to the stadium like our lives depended on it and I made it on to the terraces just as the players made their entrance.

LEE CORDEN: The day of the final was a non-stop adventure as we made our way on the train to Wembley. There were a lot more family members and friends with us than had been there throughout the FA Cup journey that started with just me and my dad for the third-round tie with Bolton.

MATT PARTRIDGE: Final day I was up very early having obtained my seat from the stubs required and a long wait in the queue. We again got the train, this time down to Euston with a bigger group of mates and made it to Trafalgar Square with four cans of Tennent's Super between 15-20 of us. I had a few swigs and felt quite charged! We made our way to Wembley and got into the ground fairly early and watched it fill. I hadn't seen that many people in one place before, it was a hugely impressive stadium.

MATT KERR: My two granddads and cousin travelled with me to Wembley. We had a champagne breakfast in a hotel near Wembley and were there by 10am. My granddads were in their sky blue blazers, I've got a great picture of them and it just sums up the whole day.

DANNY FINLAY: I went with my uncle and my mum as my dad had gone up on the Friday night. He had a pal in Harlow and they went out locally. My uncle arranged the coach with a few pals from the Walsgrave Social Club, this after my mum and I had queued for over 12 hours to get our tickets for the match. We had our five ticket stubs while my dad was a season ticket holder so it was easier for him to get a ticket. The motorway was awash with Sky Blue and we had a clear run to Wembley.

ROB SUMMERFIELD: Do you retain the superstition and go to your club's biggest ever day dressed like you're attending a wake? My mates had seemingly forewarned half the train station queue and there were roars as I joined them dark clad. This lasted until we got outside the stadium when some lass hung a scarf around my neck, I gave in then!

MOZ BAKER: I went to Wembley with my wife, her dad and a couple of other guys in the car who I'm still not sure who they were! I'd never been to a game before or after the final with them, I think they just filled the car! Each round I'd been to the games with somebody different so there were certainly no superstitions from me. We were decked in Sky Blue and the pictures look like we're off to a fancy dress party. Prior to the game I'd been on a course of acupuncture on a really bizarre diet of swede and carrot which basically involved eating nothing. I was quite skinny at the time and by the time I got to cup final day I don't know how I managed to stand for 120 minutes. I had no energy at all and ran on pure adrenalin! I ate nothing all day but in the evening I had a right skinful and was really poorly the next day. We got into the ground ridiculously early as were many others, we just wanted to savour every moment.

KEV MONKS: I was on the train which seemed to take an age to get to Wembley as I was desperate to get to the ground and get in. I had been to every City game that season, including pre-season fixtures, and there was no way I was missing out on this one. I'd heard about tickets being stolen at cup finals so took no chances, we walked round to the entrance and ran up the grass bank to the turnstiles. After queuing patiently we were inside Wembley Stadium, I'd been there for England games but this was different.

MIKE YOUNG: I was supposed to be working on cup final day and had to do a bit of subterfuge to get out of it. I just couldn't not go to the game. It was very difficult to get tickets as I didn't live in Coventry or have a season ticket. A mate of mine from Newcastle got us a couple of tickets, we drove down to Watford, parked up and got the train in. It wasn't until we got around the ground itself that we looked at the tickets properly – they were in the Spurs end! We wandered around thinking, 'What are we gonna do?' Could we swap them somehow? Unbelievably, there were a couple of Spurs fans with tickets for the Coventry end so we did a swap of semi-neutral distrust, in no-man's land, and they were perfectly valid and we were in, it was all so memorable.

FRANK PRITCHARD: In 1987 I was working for Beacon Radio covering Wolves, Villa, West Brom, occasionally Birmingham City and sometimes the Sky Blues if they were playing a Midlands rival. I'd been to the semi-final with my eldest son, Justin, but he couldn't go to the final as he had to work in the golf shop I owned so I took my youngest son to the final and we travelled up with my brother-in-law and stepfather-in-law. Tickets had been difficult to obtain but, as I had quite a few contacts, I managed to get the four we needed. Sadly, mine was apart from the others. I'd travelled up in my Sky Blue suit and was to cover the game, unofficially, for Beacon Radio. I couldn't get a press pass as the station didn't cover the Sky Blues.

GEOFF FOSTER: One of my lasting memories of the magnificent cup run was the banter between John Sillett and his mate from his playing days at Chelsea, Jimmy Greaves. 'Greavsie' was building his TV career and I reckon with a mixture of winding up his mate and a large dollop of superstition he would routinely tip Coventry's opponents as the competition progressed. Deep down, I'm sure Greaves was backing his old mucker 100 per cent. This 'rivalry' prompted what could be flatteringly titled 'a nice little earner' with the emphasis on the little! Together with a friend of mine – Dave 'you don't score runs in the pavilion' Howe – we designed and printed some Sky Blue t-shirts. The plan was to make a tidy profit knocking them out on Wembley Way...they weren't just any old product, oh no! There were cartoon images of 'Snoz' and George Curtis on the front kicking a ball (Jimmy Greaves's head) between each other. If my failing memory serves me well the cost of the cartoonist and printing/producing the clothing was just about covered by the sales.

MIKE LIGGINS: I'll never forget that moment of walking into the press box at Wembley and looking out over the pitch, it was real pinch me stuff. It was all a little bit unreal, not too clichéd to say it, but it was like a dream. I was the co-commentator for Mercia with Stuart Linnell, Kirk Stephens was our expert summariser and Paul King was there to add a little showbiz glamour.

STUART LINNELL: In those days it was the old press box at the old Wembley. It was a huge area that ran almost the length of the stand with a commentary box in the middle for the BBC partitioned and closed off from the rest of us. We were positioned at one end along with all the radio teams and it was just such an amazing view up there looking down on to the pitch. I'd been sports editor at Mercia Sound and been very much involved in sports reporting all the way through my broadcasting career so I was determined that, whatever my role, I was going to be part of the reporting/commentary team!

IAN WOODS: There was nowhere else for us to go at Wembley to watch the game. We were going to be doing the interviews around the tunnel but there was no sense in us hanging around that area while the game was ongoing, we wanted to be as close to the action as possible. In the end we were ten yards from the goal, there weren't that many photographers unlike these days where every single space behind the goal is taken. We were behind the 'MILO' hoarding at the tunnel end.

JOHN POYNTON: Prior to kick-off I went up to the official main reception, had a bite to eat and then received an official booklet which described exactly what we had to do and when on the day. My wife and I then went and sat in the Royal Box for the game. The procedure there is you sit on the front row, the two chairmen with the Duchess of Kent, myself and Tottenham's Irving Scholar. Irving sat with her for the first half while my wife and I sat next to Maggie and Denis Thatcher. It was an election year so all party leaders were visible. Neil Kinnock was also there. Denis didn't know anything about football whatsoever and what was not common knowledge was that, in the stand opposite us, they had received a security threat that something might happen at the match and had SAS with their guns at the top of the stand.

TNT had contacted us prior and asked if they could sponsor something for the FA Cup Final. We eventually suggested it could be George Dalton's physio bag and it made us quite a few thousand pounds. When 'Killer' got injured and the cameras were on him for quite a period of time, TNT got a lot of free advertising and, the Monday after the game, their HQ in Australia were so pleased with the publicity they wanted to double the amount agreed.

DANNY FINLAY: I got lost in the ground before the game started. We were in the terracing behind the goal and I'd gone to the loo but when I came back I couldn't remember which entrance it was to get back up to where my mum was. I got to the top of the entrance and it was packed on the terrace, I went back down the steps and bumped into Neil Treanor who was a friend of our family and a few years older than me. As I came down the stairs, crying, Neil grabbed hold of me and took me back up and across to where my mum was. He'd been to Wembley before so knew the layout better than me, I was a nervous wreck before the game and then we had that drama!

STEVE LEE: I went to the final with Peter Lowe. I don't know how we got the tickets but we were sat in the Spurs end.

IAN BOLTON: For the final, Paul Franks and Ian Winter did the live commentary for Radio WM with Jimmy Holmes, the former Sky Blues and Spurs player, our expert summariser. I knew Jimmy from his time as the Nuneaton Borough boss when I covered them. I was sat ten yards from Ian Woods and Rob Gurney behind the goal Coventry attacked in the first half.

IAN WINTER: I was sports editor at Radio WM and myself and Paul were sat with Jimmy Holmes, our match summariser who proved to be an inspired choice.

STEVE EVANS: I was soon to take over coverage of the Sky Blues from Neville so my brief on the day was to write a two-page feature from the fans' perspective on the terraces at Wembley to appear in the paper on the Monday. I took my place at the back of Block 69 and, as I settled in, next to me was the majority of the Coventry rugby team, a lot of them local lads and Sky Blues fans. I had to break the news to them that I would be moving to cover the Sky Blues next season.

To get paid to watch my favourite team as the chief sports writer was a dream come true, I was a season ticket holder from the age of 13 and my boyhood idol was George Hudson. Around me on the terrace I was packed in among a sea of sky blue.

STEVE COCKRILL: On the bench at Wembley I was sat next to Tottenham's Tony Galvin. I had a good bit of banter with him but I couldn't understand him half of the time with his Irish/Cockney accent!

JOHN SILLETT: My pre-match team talk focused on not conceding a goal early on. I said to the players, 'If you look at their side it is full of internationals, when they get an early goal their heads go up and away they go.' They had so many players that could turn it on. I said, 'We daren't give away an early goal, we've got to plug away and play our way and we'll play it tight.' Trevor Peake was the best defender I ever worked with, superb at reading the game. I told him, 'This is your man, you go in on Clive Allen.'

DAVID PHILLIPS: The abiding words of John when we were going out of the changing rooms were, 'Boys, I want you to enjoy yourselves.' Playing in front of 98,000, always nice, when you look at the two sides I was the only non-English player on our side with Gough, Hughton and Ossie Ardiles in their starting 11. Everyone else was English.

GRAHAM RODGER: I'll always remember the noise when we started to appear out of the tunnel when both teams came out together. The far side of the stadium sees you first so the noise starts there and then by the time the referee and captains are out the noise is deafening, 98,000 there. It was an incredible noise from both sets of fans supporting their team in the right manner.

BRIAN KILCLINE: Cyrille Regis had reached the semi-final in 1982 with West Brom when they lost after extra time to QPR. The lasting memory I have of the cup final day is of him saying to us, 'Soak it all in because it happens so quick.' You try and soak it all in but I've forgotten more than I can remember.

\\\\ \\\\ \\\\ \\\\ \\\\

City: Steve Ogrizovic; David Phillips, Brian Kilcline, Trevor Peake, Greg Downs; Dave Bennett, Michael Gynn, Lloyd McGrath, Nick Pickering; Cyrille Regis, Keith Houchen. Subs: Steve Sedgley, Graham Rodger.

Tottenham: Ray Clemence; Chris Hughton, Richard Gough, Gary Mabbutt, Mitchell Thomas; Chris Waddle, Paul Allen, Osvaldo Ardiles, Glenn Hoddle, Steve Hodge; Clive Allen. Subs: Gary Stevens, Nico Claesen.

Referee: Neil Midgley (Salford).

John Motson commentated for BBC1 with Jimmy Hill his co-commentator while on ITV Brian Moore was assisted by Ron Atkinson. The bold items in the following passages are excerpts of the day's BBC1 commentary.

JOHN MOTSON: The scene is colourful, the mood is optimistic, the stage is set for the 106th FA Cup Final, Spurs in white, that's Glenn Hoddle and Coventry in stripes, this is Keith Houchen.

2 mins: Hoddle with the kick, Gough is in there, Houchen was marking him...Clive Allen, play on says the referee, Allen seemed to use his back, it's come out again to Chris Waddle...ALLEN, CLIVE ALLEN! Would you believe it, in the second minute, goal number 49 for the Footballer of the Year, an electrifying start by Tottenham. Chris Waddle got moving, Allen came to the near post and Ogrizovic had no real chance.

In the 1982 FA Cup Final, Allen got injured in the second minute for Queens Park Rangers against Tottenham and was substituted at half-time.

JOHN SILLETT: To this day I still think it was a foul on Trevor Peake when Allen backed into him. I'm screaming 'foul' then the ball goes back out to Waddle and then we're 1-0 down. I played alongside Clive's father at Chelsea, Les, and with Clive and Paul in the side I said we've got to be on our game. It was the only mistake Neil Midgley made, he had a marvellous game and was a tremendous referee.

LLOYD McGRATH: I can recall meeting the Duchess of Kent who shook my hand and asked how I was feeling. The whole day was just so special because you dream as a kid of going to Wembley, playing in a cup final and for it to actually happen was brilliant. The amount of Coventry fans there was awesome. John's team talk, the last thing he said was, 'Don't concede early.' When they scored all the lads just looked at each other and thought, 'Bloody hell, what have we done here!' It spurred us on to get back into the game quickly.

GREG DOWNS: I've always been a 100 per cent player, I'll still have a crack and have a go and keep trying even when I'm not playing well. With Waddle you've got to keep an eye on him in the first 20 minutes, his turn to provide the cross was outstanding for Allen's goal.

NICK PICKERING: I've heard loads of managers' team talks saying, 'Keep it tight,' and played in lots of big games. John Sillett's last words were, 'Come on lads, keep it tight.' Spurs were 3/1 to win it, big favourites, all my family were there and suddenly after two minutes we're 1-0 down! I should have been a little tighter to Greg, we had a great partnership and looked after each other but it was a great ball by Waddle. You train for these moments though, you know how to handle things, if they score a second it's dangerous for us.

TREVOR PEAKE: I made the comment, tongue in cheek, when Allen scored that if we can keep it to six we'll be happy! He was my man to mark. It could have been devastating but I've always believed that you've got to be strong and I tell that to my players now [Trevor is Leicester City's lead professional development coach for the under-18 side] – they don't even know I've played in a cup final!

STEVE OGRIZOVIC: The best thing about playing Spurs in the final was to be on the same pitch as Ray Clemence who I had understudied for so many years at Liverpool. I'd been to Wembley on the bench for the 1978

European Cup Final win over Bruges and also in 1981 when Liverpool went to Paris and beat Real Madrid 1-0 with Alan Kennedy's late goal. I spent four years with him, he taught me about goalkeeping and how to play the game, all the things you need to know. I've got a lot to be thankful for being around him in that great Liverpool squad. The way that he dealt with big matches, just by watching him and talking to him, it all helped me and he was brilliant on the day in 1987. We had a chat before the game, he wished me all the best and was very generous at the final whistle – they were great words and meant a lot coming from the best goalkeeper of his generation.

DEAN EMERSON: It was a rollercoaster of a game. Going one down so early you feared the worst. Tottenham were a team of stars, Hoddle, Waddle and Ossie Ardiles.

STEVE SEDGLEY: The start was incredible. Tottenham had a hell of a team that year and got off to a flying start with Clive Allen's goal. You do fear the worst as they were a top side, one of their best in years [they finished third in the league in 1986/87].

GRAHAM RODGER: We'd gone behind so early you thought, 'Jeez, here we go,' but that was that team all over; never-say-die attitude, all in it together. There would be no one lagging behind if you left the trenches.

CHRIS HUGHTON: My biggest memory going into the game was that we were in really good form. My position was probably a little bit different to most players in our team as the majority of them had played right through the season, Clive Allen was on 48 goals and we were big favourites, more so because of the season we'd had. Once

Clive scored any apprehension and nerves at the start of the game very much disappeared as it gave us a really good start in such a massive game.

GEORGE DALTON: We had the belief and we never gave up, we all thought we'd get back into the game, it was one of those years when everything just fell into place and you don't often get that in football. We didn't get down about it and took every game as an adventure. John and George tried to keep it light-hearted but, at the same time, when it came down to the nitty gritty they were spot on. When goals went in against us we would think we'll get one back such was the mentality at the time.

ANDY TURNER: There were early fears of humiliation when Allen rattled in his 49th goal of the season with just two minutes on the clock...

MIKE YOUNG: Initial despondency when the goal went in, I remember thinking, 'This could be tricky,' but we didn't look frightened out there, we looked like we knew what we were doing and that was something about the cup run. When you saw them play they looked in control, they didn't panic even when equalisers went in or we went a goal behind.

KEV MONKS: I was still telling people City would lose when Spurs took an early lead. 'This could be a cricket score' was what many people were saying but that team bonding and togetherness instilled by George and John counted for something.

NEIL WHITE: On the day itself we drove to the match in my Allegro and I recall, after two minutes, working out how many goals Spurs could score, I thought embarrassment was inevitable.

MATT PARTRIDGE: The teams came out, the wall of sound, the colours, the songs, 'Abide With Me', everything you imagined FA Cup Final day would be about. Then, disaster struck. We were 1-0 down but this City side were made of sterner stuff, they got their collective heads up and played like they had done all season.

ROB SUMMERFIELD: I was now wearing a City scarf and within moments of the start it was self-blame as Clive Allen scored. I'd also managed to lose my friends and was watching alone. Or rather I wasn't. The songs from the hallowed terraces were like psalms in a cathedral, 'Sky Blues shooting to win'.

9 mins: JOHN MOTSON: Regis... Downs... Houchen... Bennett... DAVID BENNETT! 1-1! Look at John Sillett, they're level after nine minutes. Greg Downs curled the ball in, Houchen with the flick on, a lovely header, Clemence went down but Bennett was quicker and scored. This is the best start to an FA Cup Final for many years, Jimmy...

JIMMY HILL: It is indeed and I think when Ray Clemence looks at that at the end of the game he will think he was a little slow coming off his line, no question about that, he hesitated for a moment, Bennett was in and finished the job off.

DAVE BENNETT: I was just doing my job. When you're playing in an FA Cup Final the first thing you want to do is win the game, it's a huge bonus if you score. When I took it past Ray I was just concentrating on putting it into the back of the net. I'd played in the replayed 1981 final for Manchester City against Tottenham so had an idea what to expect and hoped my experience of those two games, sharing it with the other players, would help them. It definitely helped me because of the atmosphere and knowing it was a massive game that was the place if you were going to do anything, to perform. Back in 1981 I thought it was going to be our day when I was brought down for the penalty in the replay that Kevin Reeves converted to make it 2-1 and we were 20 minutes from winning the cup before Garth Crooks levelled and then Ricky Villa produced *that* goal to win it.

NICK PICKERING: 'Benno' scored a great equaliser just at the right time. I didn't get much of the ball that day as Paul Allen and I cancelled each other out but we worked hard as a unit and got the ball out to 'Benno' on the right. David Phillips had a great game at right-back up against Steve Hodge, he didn't give him a chance, a very under-rated player.

STEVE SEDGLEY: We got back into the game quickly and found our feet, on the day I think we deserved to win it.

MICHAEL GYNN: There was no fear for us, we'd played against the Spurs players before and it wasn't a problem for us. We'd beaten them 4-3 at Highfield Road back in December, in those days it was top level football every week, you had to be confident in your own ability. We had a good team with a lot of under-rated players. I was certainly very confident at Wembley that we would win.

IAN WOODS: When Dave Bennett equalised Rob and I both leapt up to celebrate, a moment captured in a photograph which, for many years, hung in the reception at Highfield Road. We were in prime position for that goal, literally ten yards away.

ROB GURNEY: I've always been trying to find a copy of that picture, it showed me and Ian behind the goal, leaping up with one arm in the air. The picture disappeared from Highfield Road and I don't ever know what happened to it. When I left CWR to work here at Radio WM, Geoff Foster made exhaustive enquiries as to its whereabouts for my leaving present. I used to walk by it every other week at Highfield Road when I was covering City in the King Richard Street reception. I think, for some reason, Bryan Richardson took them all down and they disappeared. It's a regret to this day that I don't have a copy.

ANDY TURNER: Thankfully 'Benno' restored parity within minutes to keep the dream alive.

ROB SUMMERFIELD: The feeling when Dave Bennett equalised was of mass relief.

MOZ BAKER: I thought we were going to get a tonking when Clive Allen scored. We'd all gone there in hope more so than expectation, they were the favourites but to concede so early on I did think, 'Are we going to get hammered today?' To bounce back as quickly as we did was just incredible.

LEE CORDEN: There was no time for tears when we went a goal down because we equalised so quickly. I could barely see the goal, the other end of the pitch felt like miles away because we were so far back in the stand with the running track around the Wembley turf adding to the distance.

MATT PARTRIDGE: Flick-on by Houchen, Bennett's in, goal for the Super Sky Blues!

30 mins: JOHN MOTSON: How nice it is to be able to say in the first half of the FA Cup Final that both teams are playing well, even the Coventry goalkeeper showing his skills...but it's gone straight to Hoddle... Peake was there, Mr Reliable,and he still hasn't got it, it's Peake again...Allen...side netting! What a dreadful moment that would have been for Ogrizovic if Glenn Hoddle could have scored, he is capable, even from that distance, if Peake hadn't been in the way it would have been a goal for Hoddle and then Clive Allen and Peake forced him wide. Double defending by Trevor Peake, much to the relief of his goalkeeper, who won't do that again. That came on the half-hour.

STEVE OGRIZOVIC: I must have been over-confident clearing it with my left foot, I should have put it into touch. As per normal my left foot let me down and I just remember in those few seconds thinking, 'What are you doing, you've just knocked the ball to probably the best player on the pitch, he's got two good feet!' Hoddle was a magnificent player, that Spurs side finished third in the league and was full of internationals who were at the top of their game. I was panicking when it landed at his feet but highly relieved it came to nothing!

TREVOR PEAKE: It was a Keystone Cops comedy moment, considering we were two of the oldest out on the pitch in sky blue the communication was not as good as it was in some of the bars we drank in down the years since we first met in 1984. We chatted a lot off the pitch but, at that particular moment, when you see the ball has fell to Clive Allen, the heart did sink at least twice and it seemed like a lifetime before the ball hit the side netting – we got away with it!

40 mins: JOHN MOTSON: Five minutes left in the first half as the Coventry anthem echoes around Wembley again although it's Spurs who have the initiative for the moment with this free kick. It'll be Hoddle to take it...and Gough's there and Mabbutt was there...AND IT'S GONE IN!...Spurs are back in front and Gary Mabbutt followed in from Richard Gough and it's 2-1. The keeper came, Gough got a touch, Mabbutt got a touch and it's crept in, it's 2-1. Spurs take the lead for the second time after 40 minutes.

TREVOR PEAKE: We had a setback just before half-time, before the game we were quite confident we could give them a game as we'd won 4-3 in the league just after Christmas and lost 1-0 at White Hart Lane. Clive Allen had scored in both fixtures and was on 48 for the season prior to kick-off. After he scored so early on it ran through my mind he was going to score a 50th that day.

KEV MONKS: We were 2-1 down at the break but I just knew that, against a Tottenham side which had been arguing about payments that led to some having 'Holsten' on their shirts and others not, this was going to be Coventry City's day.

Half-time: Coventry City 1 Tottenham Hotspur 2 Att: 98,000

JOHN POYNTON: At half-time, just the first two rows of the Royal Box go down to a private area for a cup of tea. There was a toilet there for the Duchess of Kent and when I sat next to her for the second half of the match she said to me, 'I only go in there to have a fag!' While we were in that room Margaret Thatcher was walking around at the back while Denis went to the front and asked for a gin and tonic. She cried out, 'I think a cup of tea, Denis, instead.' The Duchess of Kent was a very nice lady, she had a match programme taped to the side of her chair so she could see the players' names and next to 'Brian Kilcline' she had written 'Killer'.

JOHN MOTSON: I think we gave Gary Mabbutt that goal perhaps a little prematurely, it would appear it did go in off Brian Kilcline so it may end up being credited as an own goal but certainly Tottenham lead by two goals to one at the start of the second half.

CHRIS HUGHTON: Dave Bennett was having a fair influence on the game, although we were always confident because we had goals in the team. At 1-0 we always knew they had a chance to get back into the game and, at 2-1, his crossing influence in the game became more and more prevalent as the game progressed.

63 mins: JOHN MOTSON: Spurs now defending stoutly, this is Waddle, against Downs, across comes Peake...

['Glory, Glory, Hallelujah' rings out from the Tottenham fans behind Steve Ogrizovic's goal as he waits to kick the ball downfield]

Regis... Houchen... Bennett... HOUCHEN! BRILLIANT GOAL! Keith Houchen, the man with the midas touch in the FA Cup strikes gold for Coventry, a wonderful header! David Bennett out on the right wing against Mitchell Thomas, good cross bent in and a diving header by Keith Houchen, what a lovely goal to match the one by Allen earlier. Houchen, who a year ago, was a Scunthorpe United player watching the cup final on television in a working men's club has written his name all over the competition this season and they [camera pans to John Sillett and George Curtis] can hardly believe he's done it again for Coventry. The 63rd minute and it's 2-2 and perhaps we're in for another 4-3 after all or maybe for extra time.

Houchen's record gets better and better in cup ties, it's his fifth FA Cup goal of the season, he's only got two in the league...and Coventry have once again confounded everybody, Jimmy.

JIMMY HILL: Well, I said beforehand Spurs will know they have been in a game, and certainly both sides know they've been in a game here today. The physical element of this game for the remainder

of the time is going to really tell because it's an unusual game in many, many respects. This cup final is unusual, it's like 15, 20 years ago, we've seen humour, passion, excitement, we've seen controlled and beautiful play and that's going to tell on the players in the remainder of this game, there's no question about that. Physically, they've given 90 minutes already.

JOHN MOTSON: Well nobody will mind seeing this again. David Bennett bending the cross round Mitchell Thomas...and here comes Houchen...what about that! One to tell his children about and show them over and over again, even his grandchildren come to that, it will live in Wembley memory that goal. It's put Coventry back in the match for the second time.

JOHN MOTSON: One of my most vivid memories of the 1987 FA Cup Final was going to Coventry's hotel, The Compleat Angler, in Marlow, on the Friday prior to the game. Keith Houchen and I were sitting having a coffee and I asked him what he was doing on cup final day last year. I knew Keith from the time he had scored the winning penalty for York City against Arsenal in the 1985 FA Cup and he replied he had watched it in a working men's club in Middlesbrough. When he scored that diving header I thought how far away can you be one year and then be the centre of attention the next because that was one of the great Wembley goals. The way Coventry built the move up and Dave Bennett crossed for Keith to dive and head it in, I felt that was one of the goals I would look back on as a commentator having had the pleasure of being there and commentating on it.

KEITH HOUCHEN: You do similar things over the years as a professional but when it's on a world stage and it all comes together like it did it just makes it really special. My first thought when I laid it off to 'Benno' was to get from front post to back, that was how I'd always been coached. You're always hoping it's going to be hung up and you can either come up and attack it, which was my forte, or just get something on it.

JOHN SILLETT: The thing with 'Houchy' was that he would make a pass and watch it. I'd told him to make the pass then move to the back post. I turned to George Dalton and said, 'He's done it,' as he laid it off to Dave Bennett and moved into the box.

GEORGE DALTON: When you're watching the game from our point of view, on the bench, you don't immediately think about the quality of the goal, just that you've scored and you're now back in the game. It's only later, when you look back on it, you think, 'That was great!'

KEITH HOUCHEN: The way it worked out it's been whipped in, I'm running flat out (which wasn't that fast for me!) and I'd lost my markers. It was a matter of throwing yourself at it to get on the end of the cross and that comes back to instinct. It was all perfect timing, I was actually there in plenty of time and could watch the ball come in while I was in the air and then it's a matter of picking your spot. If there's one thought you've got it's don't miss the target, I've looked at pictures of it since (there's no pictures of it up in my house) and I could swear I've got a little smile on my face as I'm heading the ball. You can see Cyrille on the edge of the box and he's trying to head it himself, he's off the floor! It's a moment frozen in time, Chris Hughton knows it's going in, he's thrown his head back and screamed, Nick Pickering's off the floor too.

DAVE BENNETT: During the season the players would knock it out to me on the wing for me to beat the player and then it's all about me trying to deliver a ball into that area where one of our players can attack it. If you watch the goal live, see Keith Houchen's movement, he knocks it out to me and then for the first time in my life I've seen him run straight into the box (and not jogging!) to attack the space. As the season progressed I'd come back after training and cross 100 balls but, sometimes with crossing, you haven't got time to assess what's on, you've just got to put the ball into an area and that's what I did. John Sillett said to me that if you ever get the chance to cross a ball never hit it behind the goal because everybody gets upset and disappointed if you don't deliver. I never crossed balls for the keepers in training because you don't want to start crossing to them in a game. It's all about practice.

NICK PICKERING: One hundred thousand people in a football stadium and sometimes, in a match, it goes quiet. I did shout, it's amazing, we're 2-1 down and I could see the ball whipped in by Dave Bennett and I just went, 'Dive Houchy, dive!' That was one of the best goals you'll ever see. Chris Hughton's face said it all, the anguish.

CHRIS HUGHTON: As the ball came in I still couldn't see a goal, once he got his head on the ball, I knew it was in. It went from a little bit of apprehension once they got the ball into the wide area, still not so much fear once it had been crossed as I felt we would deal with it, but the despair once I knew he'd got his head on it because, I think if it had been someone else there then you might not have been thinking 'goal', but as it was Keith Houchen, who was very good at heading a ball, you knew it was going to be a goal.

KEITH HOUCHEN: It was one of the first games where they put cameras in the goal net and it captures a magical moment in time. I'd never seen myself react to scoring a goal like I did at Wembley. I just lost it. The players thought if we go chasing after him there's only so much energy you can expend in a game as big as that and on that pitch. I know 'Picks' and Micky start to chase me, I was jumping about doing all sorts of crazy stuff, god knows what I would have done if the fans had been closer to the pitch!

MICHAEL GYNN: When he scored he ran off towards the City fans and jumped over one of the advertising hoardings. I was closest to him, along with Nick, but only went so far, I'd have clattered the hoarding if I'd tried to clear it so I just let Keith go. Nick was alongside me and I said, 'Let him go, there's no way I'm leaping over that hoarding!' It was a fair distance to reach the fans and I needed to save my energy! I turned back and jogged to halfway. I remember Keith's disappointment when he looked round and nobody had gone over to celebrate with him. You have daft celebrations these days but, back then, it didn't really happen, we still had a long while to play.

NICK PICKERING: 'Houchy' is away over the boards, what people don't realise at Wembley is how lush the turf was, it was spongy and I never got cramp but in those last 20-25 minutes of normal time I was getting cramp and I was a fit lad. You could chuck your shinpads out in those days. The grass was always kept long to keep the pitch in immaculate condition and it was 80 degrees in the stadium, a wonderful day. I couldn't get after Houchy, all I was thinking was that I've got to get through the game and win the cup.

KEITH HOUCHEN: I had this massive adrenalin surge and probably paid for it later on as the legs started to lock up as they did with everybody else. It was a dream come true for me, my whole ambition from a young professional at 17 was to get to Wembley and play in a cup final. Just to get there was incredible for all of us anyway because we'd all seen the hard side of football. I'd played against most of them with my previous clubs in the lower leagues but, as the game went on, you start to think, 'We're going to win this.' You could just sense we were the better side, stronger, and were going to win it. You don't want to chase a game so getting that goal was the catalyst to spur us on.

DAVE BENNETT: I couldn't have caught Keith, I was just so ecstatic that we'd got back into the game. Dave Phillips grabbed hold of me. I knew I'd done something good but we couldn't rest on our laurels, we had to go on and win the game, concentrate and ensure we did our jobs and keep them out.

JOHN POYNTON: When Keith scored I got quite excited to the extent I jumped up and pulled the Duchess of Kent up with me. If she gets up, everyone is supposed to get up. There was a bit of consternation there and when she sat back down she said, 'I'm really pleased for you, Mr Poynton, but I'm supposed to be impartial!'

STEVE OGRIZOVIC: In my book Keith's header was the best goal ever scored at Wembley, it was a fantastic goal. I recall kicking it upfield, Cyrille headed it on and Keith knocked it out wide. Dave Bennett put a great ball in – what a goal to be scored at Wembley. It was also the best goal I saw by a Coventry player in my 601 games for the club. Maybe I'm biased. People still talk about it, John Motson spoke about FA Cup finals recently and said our final was one of the best that he'd ever seen and you listen when he speaks. A lot of people put Keith's goal right up there.

BOB HALL: 'Greavsie' said Keith Houchen's headed goal was the best he had ever seen in a cup final.

GREG DOWNS: When Houchen scored we were all too knackered to chase after him, he was off and gone. The whole thing from 'Oggy' to Cyrille to 'Benno' to in, it was an incredible goal. At the start of the second half I'd won a 50-50 with Chris Waddle and caught him unintentionally but it appeared to affect him and from then onwards we pushed him back deeper and deeper towards Chris Hughton, denied them space and moved into the ascendancy.

DAVID PHILLIPS: I've only watched the final two or three times in its entirety since 1987. I was a long way behind Keith when the ball came in from 'Benno' and you can see me skip as he heads it and then, when it went in, utter elation. I don't even think I got to him, I went over to 'Benno'. It was a fantastic goal, well worked, a fantastic cross and, as Keith says, he never closed his eyes. 'You've gotta dive for it' and the rest is history.

LLOYD McGRATH: What a goal that was. Keith's header was a fairytale goal. The game was fantastic, end-to-end, an open game, proper football.

JOHN SILLETT: It was the best header I've ever seen. All through my career I can't recollect seeing a better headed goal. Jimmy Greaves was the greatest goalscorer I ever played alongside but he only scored two with his head!

TREVOR PEAKE: It was a great goal but the importance of it at the time was crucial. It was vital we got back in the game after we'd had the setback just prior to half-time.

GRAHAM RODGER: 'Benno' was on fine form at Wembley while it was pure 'Roy of the Rovers' with Houchen, what a goal, one of the best ever. If that had been Eden Hazard crossing for Fernando Torres you'd be seeing that goal over and over again, it was world-class. People would stand up and applaud that in any stadium.

STEVE COCKRILL: Houchen didn't use his boots to score the header, mind, I took praise for the fact his boots were so comfortable he got to the ball with his diving header! I'm not taking anything away from the cross by 'Benno' either!

NEVILLE FOULGER: One of the great goals at Wembley. Again, you half-expected that header from him because he'd had that run through the cup ties of scoring vital goals. There are marvellous photos of that header, it was a great moment. I think everybody went to Wembley with the feeling, 'We might not win it but it will be a great day out,' but, deep down, you hoped they would come up trumps.

STUART LINNELL: For a split second I think we all held our breath and thought, 'What have we just seen?' It has to be one of the all-time special goals in any competition and, bearing in mind we'd been through the opening few minutes with Tottenham scoring, to come back in the way we did and for him to score like that was just extraordinary.

IAN WINTER: I thought that Jimmy Holmes, having played for both clubs, he'd give us a balanced view of the match. How wrong I was! Jimmy, a very articulate, softly-spoken Irishman, greeted Keith Houchen's header by leaping into the air, shouting at the top of his voice!

IAN WOODS: I was so far away, behind the Coventry goal, that it was only when I saw TV replays later that evening I realised it was a diving header!

ROB GURNEY: It was way in the distance and you couldn't see/tell how fantastic a goal it was until we saw the replay afterwards.

MIKE LIGGINS: I can remember Houchen's goal well as it was the only one I commentated on as Stuart got all the others!

MATT PARTRIDGE: People around me were getting anxious as the second half progressed, myself included, with the exception of one of my mates, John Baxter, who was adamant we were going to score and I put some of the victory down to him! With 'we're gonna score in a minute' booming out from the Sky Blue faithful Oggy kicked downfield. It was expertly flicked on by Cyrille to

Benno out on the wing. He took a couple of touches before curling in the best cross and there was big Keith, flying like a salmon, to head it past Ray Clemence. What a goal, what a top goal! He then came running towards us in Block D and after all these years when I see the goal repeated I always remember this! The man of the moment!

NEIL WHITE: At this point I began to worry that the match would finish 2-2 because I had a new job at the *Birmingham Post and Mail* and didn't know whether I would get time off for the replay!

KEV MONKS: It will always be my favourite goal scored by a City player. It was a moment of brilliance and one that brought so much hope.

FRANK PRITCHARD: Keith wasn't a prolific scorer but that cross was brilliant and it was 'Roy of the Rovers' stuff. You look back at Robin van Persie's diving header for Holland in last year's World Cup, that was similar. You can go to football matches most of your life and not be fortunate enough to be there when a goal like that is scored. People were sat either side of me as I was speaking into my Motorola brick. I had use of one of the first ever mobile phones as I reported on the game for Beacon Radio, it must have been strange for the fans around me!

MOZ BAKER: It seemed like the ball was in the air for such a long time. You could see where it was heading for. There was such elation around us, amazement and disbelief at such a brilliant goal. That was one of the defining moments of all my time supporting Coventry City. I actually took a tape recorder with me on to the terrace to play on the show we did and I'm desperately trying to find it as there's so much good stuff on there, it's quite unique. I remember listening back to it on the way home and to hear the songs from the terraces was simply fantastic.

ROB SUMMERFIELD: That moment, being perfectly positioned, right in line behind the goal when Houchen entered football folklore. For some reason there were a few Spurs fans standing by me in our end. 'I'm not having that,' uttered one of them in disbelief at what he'd just witnessed.

75 mins: JIMMY HILL: Many will come off this field today with credit, none more so than Neil Midgley, the referee, who has played his part in the players' exhaustion because he's refused to blow up unless he's seen a positive foul, he's kept the game flowing beautifully to the enjoyment of everybody.

85 mins: JOHN MOTSON: This is Mabbutt...foul... Brian Kilcline hurt himself as well as Gary Mabbutt.

BRIAN KILCLINE: Earlier on in the game I had the same scenario. Gary Mabbutt had broken through, played a one-two, went past me and got a shot in. The reason I did what I did, harping on back to my earlier years, I was taught how to play the game and remembered that you can let one past but not both. So the ball goes past and I caught Gary but I caught him wrong, he caught me and I've gone down. I knew I'd messed up and referee Neil Midgley called me over, he could see that I was hurt and said, 'What the hell are you doing a tackle like that for?' I can't remember my response but then ran back to my position to try and shake off the knock, at which point my leg had doubled in size. That's when the pain started and I had to come off.

88 mins: JOHN MOTSON: There's going to be the first substitution of this cup final and Graham Rodger, who wasn't even in the squad until this time yesterday, will replace Brian Kilcline, hobbling after his somewhat reckless challenge on Gary Mabbutt.

JIMMY HILL: And Trevor Peake regains the captaincy that he lost to an argument with a previous manager.

GRAHAM RODGER: I'm on the bench enjoying the game with one of the best seats in the ground watching a fantastic, intriguing game. People say were you nervous but I wasn't because of Sill's brilliant managerial skills keeping me calm beforehand. I'm forever indebted because when I went on in the 88th minute I wasn't worried about going on. 'Killer' never went down, never ever stayed down, I started to think, 'Hang on a minute.' Sedge was on the bench with me and he had played some games at centre-half and then George said, 'You're going on.' I remember running past 'Killer' and, as we were defending a corner, I asked him, 'Who have you got?' He replied 'Mabbutt' through clenched teeth, he was in so much pain from the tackle he made. I went on and actually won the first header from that corner and thought, 'Here we go.'

STEVE SEDGLEY: I had a feeling Graham would go on when 'Killer' went down injured. He had been playing recently, got into the team at the back end of the season and had played well. He was a natural replacement at the time because I was playing a bit more in midfield. I was disappointed and still am to this day but I wasn't surprised I didn't go on to replace 'Killer'. The lads gave me a lot of ribbing afterwards saying I didn't deserve a medal as I didn't play! You don't want to change things, like the semi-final, it it's not broken, that kind of scenario. Those kind of decisions earn the manager his money and the decision proved right. I had a fantastic first year at Coventry but it was so disappointing not to get on at Wembley because that's what you dream of. I was fortunate enough to return in 1991 with Tottenham when we beat Forest 2-1.

GEORGE DALTON: Being the sort of lad he was, Brian wanted to carry on but he obviously couldn't. The next day I took him to see the specialist surgeon and then on the Monday he had an operation to remove the blood clot.

BRIAN KILCLINE: I sat on the bench for the remainder of the game next to the club doctor who was chain-smoking throughout to calm his nerves. It was like watching the cup final back home in your local pub, all that was missing was a pint!

Full time: Coventry City 2 Tottenham Hotspur 2 – extra time to follow

LLOYD McGRATH: Prior to extra time John instructed us to stand up and told us we were fitter than Spurs who were sat on the floor.

GRAHAM RODGER: It was a really hot day, the game was at times quite slow but I think that's the pitch and the atmosphere/occasion. It goes into extra time and I'm looking around thinking, 'We look all right here.' I'd not seen anyone flagging.

NICK PICKERING: John Sillett got everyone going before extra time, his team talk was fantastic.

DAVE BENNETT: We were a fit side, George played a masterstroke before extra time, saying, 'Don't sit down, don't lie down, don't let them see you're tired, make sure you're on your toes.' We didn't want to give them any psychological advantage.

IAN WOODS: At the end of normal time I tried to walk round the pitch to the halfway line to describe John Sillett and George Curtis talking to the players, trying to lift them for extra time. I was in full flow when a Wembley official tried to usher me back behind the advertising hoardings. As I meekly obeyed, I tripped and fell but carried on commentating!

95 mins: JOHN MOTSON: Just over five minutes gone in the first period of extra time...this is Graham Rodger...did that beautifully...

GRAHAM RODGER: The irony of the pass to Lloyd is Glenn Hoddle knocks a decent ball into Paul Allen, he had a half-bad touch which allowed me to nick it off him and in the peripheral view I can see Nick Pickering wide on the left. I've had a glance up and thought 'glory ball' and, for some reason, I took another touch and then the picture changed and opened up the other view to Lloydy and now it's on my left foot which was never very good and didn't get much better. I had the confidence to have a swing at it and his first touch takes him on and now he's in behind them out on the right wing. It was a rather fortunate pass really as I so nearly went for the glory ball to Nick.

JOHN MOTSON: ...and it's McGrath, Pickering's in the centre, Regis joining him...

LLOYD McGRATH: I can't remember how I ended up on the right wing when Graham Rodger picked me out with his pass. I found myself out there and raced towards goal.

NICK PICKERING: When Lloyd went down the wing I'm breaking my neck to get into the box...

JOHN MOTSON: ...ohhhh Mabbutt, IT'S AN OWN GOAL!...Gary Mabbutt put it in, Lloyd McGrath gets the congratulations, it's one of those that he just inadvertently deflected...McGrath went down the line, he curled it in for a cross and Mabbutt, that has to be an own goal, it changed the whole direction of the ball and beat Ray Clemence and Mabbutt, who may have forced a similar goal at the other end is now victim of one which puts his team behind...what a devastating moment for this fine player but what a delightful one for the Coventry fans because their team are in front for the first time.

JIMMY HILL: And what an extraordinary thing, Rodger, who came on, made that pass to McGrath who's not renowned as a goalscorer but has scored three goals recently for them, the local boy who made good and has put them in the lead at Wembley.

LLOYD McGRATH: When I crossed it I thought it was going to go out for a corner, it seemed to take forever from when it hit Gary's knee to when it dropped into the goal. I just couldn't believe it. I'd looked up when I ran down the wing and could only see Nick Pickering running into the box. I've tried to pick him out and Gary Mabbutt's knee got in the way of the ball and it looped up. I just thought, 'Wow!' When it went over Ray Clemence, it was just crazy, I couldn't believe what had happened, it was a fantastic feeling!

NICK PICKERING: I still have dreams now of the ball coming back off the crossbar and me smacking it in! It was right in the top corner, I was so close to it and thought it was going to come off the bar. It was fantastic!

ROB GURNEY: I can visualise it now from where I was sitting, when Lloyd McGrath's cross hit Mabbutt's knee, and thinking the minute it struck him, 'I know where this is going!' It looped and looped, Clemence couldn't get there and it bounced in. We were at the end where all the Tottenham fans were, it was a muted atmosphere around us but I'm sure I was on my feet with fists in the air! I recall Clemence went up to Mabbutt and tried to console him, it seemed surreal, didn't feel right at the time, one of those moments where life is going on around you but doesn't seem real.

IAN BOLTON: There is a photo that used to be at Highfield Road, along with the one depicting the scenes after Dave Bennett's goal, in a corridor, of the winning goal. I'm on the left behind the 'MILO' hoarding then Ian Woods has his arms raised next to Rob Gurney who has his left arm in the air.

GEORGE DALTON: You wouldn't get anyone who would give more than Lloyd did for the team over the years. Quite often he would play when he wasn't 100 per cent fit, he did have a lot of injuries but he was one of the old school and soldiered on. For the final to finish as it did with him involved in the winning goal was brilliant for him. He gave 100 per cent every game, he never knew when he was beaten. His attitude was fabulous and he was a lovely lad, he'd battle for everything. Lloyd would be the first to admit he wasn't the best on the ball but, in terms of tackling and winning the ball back for you, he was great.

GRAHAM RODGER: Along with the noise when we emerged from the tunnel at the start of the game I always remember when I ended up in the left-back position with Chris Waddle running at me. I end up one-on-one and can hear the tension in the Coventry supporters close to me as the young lad was up against Waddle. He dropped his shoulder to go past me but I slid in left-footed and knocked the ball out of play and got a huge roar from the fans.

113 mins: JOHN MOTSON: Seven minutes separating them from the trophy...Spurs, never beaten in an FA Cup Final, I know we keep saying that but it is one of the most enduring records in the game at stake here.

IAN BOLTON: In the second half of extra time Steve Ogrizovic turned to me and said, 'Ian, how much longer?' There weren't any clocks in the stadium. I think I told him 'five or six minutes'. As victory was getting closer the time ticked slower! I was asked to describe on air just how much the ball had looped up off Gary Mabbutt, as you can see I got a pretty good view of it! You'd never get to sit on the grass by the goal at the FA Cup Final now!

116 mins: JOHN MOTSON: Coventry have got to steer their way through another four minutes... Bennett, looks for Gynn and he might finish it here, it's Michael Gynn for Coventry, he's gone round Clemence who saved brilliantly!

MICHAEL GYNN: Dave played me through in the last few minutes of extra time, I've gone past Gary Stevens and tried to chip it over Ray Clemence and my legs just gave way on me. He then booted it long and my first thought was that I would have to get back into midfield – if I'd made it 4-2 it would have been game over and I could have scored the winning goal in the FA Cup final. The most important thing was to win the game.

DAVE BENNETT: I said to Micky, 'I'd have had man of the match if you'd scored then!'

120 mins: JOHN MOTSON: Neil Midgley has looked across at the linesman on our side of the field, this could be the last attack, it's Hoddle, it's Paul Allen, it's Claesen now for Tottenham, in stoppage time. Neil Midgley looks again...Stevens...Waddle... Coventry have got to keep their shape, Spurs have got to press it in with Hodge...Hoddle...it's Ogrizovic's ball! Probably the most excited George Curtis has been all afternoon, just look at John Sillett, he knows how close they are to glory, unheard of before in Coventry's history...AND THAT'S IT! IT'S COVENTRY CITY'S FIRST MAJOR TROPHY IN 104 YEARS AND TOTTENHAM HOTSPUR HAVE BEEN BEATEN IN AN FA CUP FINAL FOR THE VERY FIRST TIME!...David Pleat...numb by

what's happened, George Curtis and John Sillett elated, Coventry's name was on the cup after all and there are one or two players who still can't believe it, the management team can and the supporters certainly do.

JIMMY HILL: It's a proud moment for me too to see people like George and John enjoying this wonderful time. I don't know when I've enjoyed a game of football as much.

JOHN SILLETT: At the final whistle David Pleat said, 'I couldn't have lost to a nicer fella' – we were big mates, Pleaty and I. My father-in-law owned the fish market in Coventry. David Pleat loved his fish and I always promised him that if we ever met in a big match, if we won, I would get him a box of fish. He said, 'I'll be waiting for the fish' – which I have never delivered! For me, David Phillips was an unsung hero on the day, he went into the right-back position, a position he didn't really enjoy, and did it for the sake of the club. He was a tremendous athlete and did a great job for us.

GEORGE DALTON: There was sheer relief when the whistle blew, to get so far, it was a heck of a cup run and we were counting down the seconds on the touchline.

CYRILLE REGIS: The final whistle was the sweetest sound in the world. You've been in football so long but until that whistle blows it's not over. That whistle at 3-2, you've hung on, the soft Wembley turf, you're absolutely wrecked, as a kid this is what you've always wanted, you've done it, you're there and you've won, you just cannot wait for that last whistle. For a team like Coventry, we've won nothing for 104 years, to be part of that legacy is just awesome, especially because I left West Brom for Coventry and it didn't work out for two years. I was in the wilderness, didn't perform well, didn't play well, it was an absolute nightmare in terms of form and being an England player – it was a bit redemptive for me. It was a great adventure for us all and no one expected us to win.

It was a similar game to the 4-3 at Christmas, it went back and forth until we won it in the end. The 4-3 showed we had the character to beat Tottenham, we came back twice at Wembley, 1-0, 2-1 down and Lloyd McGrath, whose job was to man-mark Hoddle all game, was a really fit lad who found himself in loads of space on the right wing, crosses it, off Mabbutt's knee, I don't care how it goes in and we won the cup – fantastic!

LLOYD McGRATH: I was given a job to do in the final, to keep Glenn Hoddle quiet. I think I did that quite well. Being involved in the final goal was a brilliant memory. I went around breaking up the play and had loads of energy. Glenn was a great player and I was just glad that he didn't have too much influence on the game that day.

NEVILLE FOULGER: It was the greatest day in Coventry City's history and remains so. I was with them from 1973–1987 and the number of times I covered them just avoiding relegation… so to finish on such a high note was incredible. The 3-2 prediction I made prior to the game was probably the best one I ever made! In 1987 the FA Cup was still one of the national treasures as it hadn't been diluted by the start of the Premier League. It was such a massive occasion to everyone in those days, no one fielded weakened sides back then but it all changed in 1992.

I had to give Lloyd McGrath a ten in my match report, there was no other way of doing it on the day. I didn't give out many tens, plenty of fours, fives and sixes over the years which didn't go down at all well at times but it was the complete team performance at Wembley. It was in the top five cup finals, I still consider it to be one of the best. Clive Allen's stunning header could have been the killer blow but to come back twice just showed the battling spirit. I think a lot of it was down to John Sillett and George Curtis, no doubt about that, they put a team together that were prepared to run through brick walls.

I began my career at the *Nottingham Evening Post* in 1956. You look back at your own great memories and covering the Wembley final is right up among them. One of the others I place high is interviewing Cassius Clay and that was a terrific thrill.

GREG DOWNS: I still maintain we were the better side on the day. You have to remember 'Gynny' missed two one-on-ones and we had Cyrille's header disallowed which I thought was harsh. 'Oggy' hasn't had any great saves to make, he had a couple of long-range efforts from Waddle but not too much else. Ray Clemence was by far the busier keeper. Little old Coventry beat the mighty Spurs, it was 11 versus 11 and we fancied ourselves against them as we'd beaten them 4-3 and lost 1-0 at their place when we absolutely murdered them.

MICHAEL GYNN: When you've played for 120 minutes you're tired, it was a hot day and we never took fluid on board like is the norm now, every player on the pitch would have been dehydrated. It was a fantastic feeling but it's not until later that you realise, 'I've just won the FA Cup!'

KEITH HOUCHEN: The Spurs players were very gracious at the final whistle. I vaguely recall Chris Waddle saying, 'You deserved to win it.' I looked up at the sky when Neil Midgley blew the final whistle, trying to get it all to sink in that I had just won the FA Cup because it was such a massive competition then compared to what it is now. The whole stadium stayed in, nobody left, we got applauded off just as much by the Tottenham fans. It was one of those games, a special one, and you appreciated it for what it was. We did a full lap of the stadium and I've been at cup finals recently where the whistle goes and it empties at the losing end. It also happened in the semi-final with the Leeds supporters, they all stayed in and we did a lap of honour. We didn't hold back in any way, shape or form in the final.

PAUL CULPIN: I was sat in the stand with Dean Emerson after I'd been called up on the Friday into the 16-man squad when Brian Borrows went into hospital. I wasn't initially due to travel to Wembley until the day of the game. When we were losing 1-0 you think, 'We're going to get hammered here,' but to come back and win 3-2 was unbelievable. We were massive underdogs with the players Tottenham had. To be walking out at Wembley with the suit on was a great memory for me. We were sat on the halfway line near to the dugout area. There was such a great atmosphere and everybody was off their feet when we scored. It was a great memory for me even though I wasn't on the pitch just to be involved in the whole occasion.

DEAN EMERSON: We tried to get down on to the pitch to join the lads but Wembley staff wouldn't let us!

TERRY GIBSON: I watched the game in Malta, two of my former teams in the final. I am so grateful, every season the cup final is on television, I sit there with a warm heart knowing I played in one and won [Wimbledon's 1-0 victory against Liverpool in 1988]. That feeling will apply to the Coventry players, I see David Phillips nearly every weekend at Sky on the Spanish football and the FA Cup often comes up in conversation. Coventry won it in style, at Wimbledon we won against the odds against a big team. For different reasons they were both memorable finals.

IAN WOODS: When Neil Midgley blew his whistle for the final time I was describing the scenes of celebration and told that I'd have to do the commentary on City lifting the trophy. The Royal Box was positioned directly underneath the commentary position which meant Mike and Stuart couldn't actually see the moment that Coventry fans had waited a century for. Looking back now, I wished I'd prepared something poetic to say. I'm sure John Motson had rehearsed his 'Sky Blues are sky high' comment as Brian Kilcline picked up thc trophy. I listen back to the commentary now on the audio recording 'Sky Blue Magic' and my words sound totally inadequate to describe such an historic moment.

LLOYD McGRATH: Walking up the steps to the Royal Box I kept talking to myself, saying, 'I can't believe this is happening.' To go up the steps and when 'Killer' picked up the FA Cup and held it aloft it was just fantastic!

BRIAN KILCLINE: With my leg as it was that was a lot of steps. When I got to the top of those steps I knew our name was on the cup. As I picked up the cup it was typical me with a few expletives, I kissed the cup and cried out, 'You f****** beauty!'

DAVE BENNETT: I was one of the last to go up the steps to the Royal Box as I was shaking every Tottenham player's hand. I'd played against Glenn Hoddle, Ossie Ardiles and Chris Hughton in the 1981 final and just had the biggest smile after losing to them six years previously but it was all done in a sportsmanlike fashion.

STEVE COCKRILL: At what point did I decide to go on the pitch and join the players in their pitchside photo? I cannot answer that question, it was just the emotion of the day. I'm sat on the bench at Wembley, in the third row with Neil Sillett and Tony Galvin either side, Mick Coop was next to Neil and Mark Bowen and John Chiedozie next to Galvin. Emotions took over and next thing I was in the team picture on the Wembley pitch! After the game, back in the dressing room, they had a big bath and I dived in with the lads. John Sillett tore a strip off me, I remember that – he was only joking – it was absolutely brilliant! They had to hold me back from going up to the Royal Box!

STEVE SEDGLEY: Steve Cockrill was the lucky charm, he was a good lad and must have had a great time!

KEITH HOUCHEN: He was really smart – he jumped on all the pictures after the final whistle!

BOB HALL: If you recall the television pictures as Messrs Sillett and Curtis rightly took their bow for their splendid achievement – FA Cup in hand on a tour of the ground – 'Schnoz' grinning and waving the trophy, caught by TV and photographers alike, to Jimmy Greaves in the ITV commentary box. It needed no words. Jimmy knew it was for him – taking the pair back to their Chelsea days when the wise old full-back took the young soon-to-be-star under his wing.

JIMMY GREAVES: Love 'Schnoz'! Always a great mate and he did a superb job to guide Coventry to that victory.

GARY NEWBON: When Coventry won it, John Sillett, who has always been a big mate of mine, was doing a dancing jig underneath the ITV box with George Curtis and the cup as Jimmy Greaves and him were huge mates. They played together at Chelsea and funnily enough, later on John became one of my co-commentators at Central TV on our live matches. We go back a long way. Coventry were the underdogs that day. It was one of the best cup finals of all time, so exciting. They are not normally that good.

Coventry were a good side, there was a great spirit among the players and they still have reunions. With modern teams you won't get that camaraderie because you've got Argentines, Spanish, Italians and they all disappear afterwards. No Midlands team has won the FA Cup since. I used to joke Margaret Thatcher had picked Highfield Road for training the British astronauts as there was no atmosphere but the cup run killed that one! It was a fantastic achievement, Sillett and Curtis were good fun and the team was full of characters.

IAN WOODS: Just as I had after the semi-final I was allowed into the dressing room afterwards to interview the players. This was a rare honour. Even now, journalists seldom get into the inner sanctum but being the reporter from the Coventry local radio station I was welcomed inside to join the celebrations. The person we all wanted to hear from initially was John Sillett. Bear in mind the TV guys had the priority doing the post-match interviews with BBC and ITV so everybody else had to hang around and wait. John came out from the TV interview room and went straight into a live interview with me for Mercia and then Stuart came down from the commentary box where he had been with Mike Liggins and arrived just after I had started the interview.

I looked over to him and thought, 'I bet he wishes he was doing this interview!' but I was in the middle of the interview with John and then, after that, I went into the dressing room. I interviewed John Poynton which was an unusual thing to happen on cup final day, to interview the chairman in the dressing room!

JOHN POYNTON: Winning the cup was fantastic. After the game I went down to the dressing room and did a couple of interviews for TV and radio.

ROB GURNEY: We all ended up in the dressing room and, to this day, I've still got a couple of champagne corks that I kept. Only I know what they are and it makes it special to know where they came from. Everybody was just spent by then, physically and emotionally, just gawping at each other, scarcely able to believe what happened. I also kept the yellow press bibs with 'Football Association 18' on it as a souvenir of the day and my age at the time. Fantastic times. I thought it would be the start of something special and, it never, for whatever reason, materialised.

IAN WOODS: In between interviews I was even allowed to hold the FA Cup. I went back to just five years previous as a schoolboy in Belfast watching the cup final on TV with my dad as we did every year. My dad died in 1986, if only he could have seen me at Wembley. Many of the players were singing in the communal bath when they saw me pointing my microphone at them to record the sound. Spontaneously they broke into 'one Brian Borrows, there's only one Brian Borrows' which brought a lump to my throat.

All the key interviews with John Sillett, Dave Bennett, Lloyd McGrath and Brian Kilcline had been done, the players were getting dressed and heading out towards the coach but I still hadn't spoken to 'Houch' who'd been much in demand with the national newspaper reporters. I finally interviewed him as we walked along through the Wembley concourse towards the coach as the stadium staff were clearing up. He was so happy. Before the final he'd told me he'd probably faint if he scored. He didn't faint but he was still pinching himself that his dream had come true. I wish I had more photographic memories of 1987. In those days we didn't have camera phones, you had to physically take a camera with you. I didn't have one at Wembley or at any of the matches leading up to it. The only thing I have got is a scarf which is a 'Cup Winners' one. I also have a Mercia Sound cup winners t-shirt after Mercia craftily printed a whole load of them several days before the final took place and flogged them for some outrageous sum on the streets of Coventry on the Sunday.

STEVE EVANS: I stayed behind after the final whistle and can recall two or three Coventry kids sat on the terraces who didn't want to go home, they wanted to savour every last moment. There were blue and white helium balloons in the stadium rafters, those balloons wouldn't come back down to earth and symbolically reflected the mood in the Sky Blue camp. The stadium cleaning guys came round and said we were welcome back any time although the balloons would still be there in August when we would return for the Charity Shield. The photographers who we had there had to rush out of Wembley to our van, develop their film in a darkroom and then send their pictures back to Coventry to get them printed for *The Pink*. We had to have two *Pinks* that day as the paper was usually out at 5pm on a matchday. When the game went into extra time we brought out a second edition with a massive picture of 'Killer' on the front.

ANDY SCAYSBROOK: All I can say is that I have never experienced such a joyous and emotional two hours and I'm sure I never will again. The absolute bedlam that broke out when 'Killer' lifted the cup was beyond anything I had ever witnessed before or sadly since. The sunlight catching the old pot as 'Killer' lifted it into the air like some conquering Viking was – until the birth of my son – the most emotional moment of my life.

ANDY TURNER: It was a classic that took each and every City fan through the full gamut of emotions. The euphoric feeling at the final whistle was a one-off, never to be repeated as father, son and best mate hugged, cheered and shed the odd tear.

ROB SUMMERFIELD: 'Killer' making that rush-of-blood tackle stood out for me. No thought of personal safety, just sheer commitment. When he lifted the cup it was the realisation of a dream, a fantasy made real by hard work and refusal to accept defeat.

KEV MONKS: When Lloyd McGrath's cross hit Gary Mabbutt's knee and went in I was hugging people I had never met in my life and they were doing the same. When the whistle blew, that was it. I was in tears, the emotion of it all had got to me in a way that nothing has before or since and I never actually saw 'Killer' lift the cup.

NEIL WHITE: Afterwards we were shellshocked. Spurs fans were asking why we were so glum, I replied that we'd never had reason to celebrate winning anything before!

LEE CORDEN: It felt like we stayed inside Wembley for hours after the game. I slept most of the way home but woke to see them selling a souvenir edition of *The Pink* when we got back to Coventry station.

MATT PARTRIDGE: Absolute dreamland! I'll be forever happy that my City, my Sky Blues won the 1987 FA Cup. No one will ever be able to take that away from us.

MATT KERR: My cousin owned the coach we were travelling on and on the way home we took out the skylights and sat on the roof going down the Walsgrave Road. I'll never forget it, a fabulous time. Everyone was hanging off the bridges as we arrived back into Coventry, you get goose pimples talking about it even after all these years.

DANNY FINLAY: We hadn't seen my dad all weekend and this was long before mobile phones. At the end of the game, after 'Killer' had lifted the cup, all you could see was the cup shining and glinting in the sun, the terrace started to clear and my mum had said to wait for a few minutes to let the numbers disperse. It's by now 30 minutes after the final whistle and I looked to my left and 20 or 30 yards away, sat on the terrace steps were my dad and his two best mates crying their eyes out. It was so surreal. We didn't go home with him, he went off and was out again that night. The camaraderie on that terrace was something else and it must have geed the players up. As a player you can sense the atmosphere and it can galvanise. The scenes after Houchen's goal were unreal, it was unbelievable. The goal was spectacular. Dave Bennett did what he did best, gave himself half a yard on Mitchell Thomas then put the ball on a sixpence for him.

MOZ BAKER: After the semi and final we went to the Tiger Moth pub in Ernesford Grange. It was a cracking night and after the semi-final, Tony Dobson, who'd made his debut back in the spring at Villa Park, was in there on everyone's shoulders. They were great nights.

MIKE LIGGINS: The clearest memory I have is after the game going back up the M1 and seeing a load of cars with scarves and everybody beeping their horns. At that moment I said to Ian Woods (we had a recorded programme planned for that night) that we'd be mad not to be on air tonight.

IAN WOODS: As we neared Coventry we could see fans standing on the motorway bridges waving to the returning supporters. There was a city-wide party going on and, even though we thought we'd finished work for the day, we wanted to carry on with the celebrations.

MIKE LIGGINS: We called Stuart and he said to just go on air. We played 'Go For It, City' about ten times and had people on the phone while Ian played all the interviews he had made after the final whistle. It was one of the most memorable broadcasts I ever did, just Ian and I. I can't recall what time we came off air. It was completely off the cuff and, even though I say it myself, completely brilliant!

STUART LINNELL: The players didn't want to talk to the national media afterwards, like Wimbledon the following year after their win against Liverpool, as they'd been written off, but said they would go on *Match of the Day* because it was Jimmy Hill there. We stayed until the players left and were the last people from Coventry to leave the stadium. The players went off to their party in Rugby and we drove back down the motorway. There were fans everywhere, on the bridges, flags hanging off them, and we got back to Coventry down the Walsgrave Road and people were everywhere. They were all dancing outside the pubs, they even coloured the beer sky blue, cheering whoever drove past. I spoke with Mike and Ian and told them to play 'Go For It, City' over and over as they were all singing along to it. We had a link back to the studio and it was just incredible.

STEVE COCKRILL: We went back to Rugby and that was a good night. After the game we had stayed at Wembley for a bit and were taken off to the BBC interview room with Jimmy Hill.

JOHN POYNTON: We left Wembley and made our way to the Brownsover Hall Hotel in Rugby which we had hired for the evening. We went in two coaches, the team and directors in one and the ladies in the other. Going back up the motorway it seemed every bridge we went under there were people shouting and waving flags, celebrating and cars beeping their horns. We got to Rugby and there were cameramen around camped in the hedgerows to take pictures. Our room was above the dancefloor where the music was still thumping away at 3am. We had booked the whole hotel and, as a result, everybody else staying there had been cancelled with the exception of one couple who had got married and they had not cancelled their reservation. We looked after them and they certainly remembered their wedding day!

JENNY POOLE: It was an amazing and unforgettable experience, all of that hard work and long hours had been worth it. We returned to Coventry and drove home to change for the celebrations at the team hotel. The journey from the railway station to home took forever, the roads were lined with hundreds of people wearing Sky Blue, all waving and cheering. Car horns were tooting and no one took any notice of the traffic lights. We eventually made it to the hotel where everyone was jubilant and we drank champagne from the FA Cup.

STEVE EVANS: We stopped off on the way home in Oxfordshire at an old pub for a pint then headed back to Coventry. Ten miles or so outside the city people were waving Sky Blue flags at the side of the road, a crazy, lovely atmosphere. The paper was bringing out a special on the Monday so Roger and I went back to the office until around 11.30pm when we went over to the Town Wall Tavern by the Belgrade Theatre which was packed with supporters. The Belgrade water was blue, it was just a fabulous experience.

Roger Draper passed away about four years ago. He was a fabulous writer who stayed loyal. His words were grass roots and he had a great turn of phrase. He was the best wordsmith I ever worked with. At his funeral John Sillett was there and his casket left the service to the music of *Sports Report.*

IAN WINTER: For me, the abiding memory of that incredible weekend will be those amazing scenes on that long drive home. All along the route, thousands upon thousands of Sky Blues fans celebrated their famous victory. Never before has the M1 staged the mother of all parties. Scarves, flags, banners were draped from every motorway bridge and, back in Coventry, the party went on...and on...and on, an unforgettable end to a grand day out.

JIM BROWN: Inside Wembley I had a great seat with my wife, Doreen, close to the massed end of City fans, thankfully surrounded by Sky Blues supporters. After the game I was exiting the seated area, looked up to the higher stands and spotted my best friend Michael May, with his father. Michael was a very fair weather fan – I can't remember him attending a City game in the previous five years – his father never went! Ever since Michael and I have given him stick that he probably deprived two far more deserving fans of a seat at Wembley! That day will forever be one of the greatest of my life.

STEVE LEE: It was such an amazing game, it was a triumph in many ways against big money and sponsorship as Spurs had had a row over which shirts they would wear and Coventry were just delighted to be there. They weren't multi-million pound players but they had more about them in wanting to win. The Houchen header and the ecstatic scenes at full time, as we were driving back there were people dancing in the Belgrade fountain.

NEIL WHITE: On our return we were amazed by how many fans were cheering on the motorway bridges and when we drove into Coventry. I stopped at a traffic light outside the Sir Colin Campbell pub and was offered a drink from a stranger after he asked if we had been to Wembley – that just doesn't happen! It was as if we were the conquering heroes. I had offered to cover the Sunday homecoming for the *Birmingham Post* who I had joined the week previously.

NEIL JONES: Most people had to wait years to see the Sky Blues win the FA Cup. I had to wait seven months! My first game was a 1-0 win over Wimbledon in October 1986 when Dave Bennett scored and Dean Emerson made his debut. The referee that day was Neil Midgley. I remember walking to the ground holding my dad's hand, all excited, and fell in love instantly with our club and football. As a five-year-old, back in 1987, I don't think I fully understood the impact it would have on people. We've all probably watched the game many times over the years but I can honestly say I haven't felt such sheer joy and happiness since that wonderful day.

ROB SUMMERFIELD: Back in my local, The Bulls Head, on the Binley Road, I leant on the bar taking it all in. The songs, the colours, the emotion, a rich Sky Blue tapestry with an angelic soundtrack, slightly tinged with black of course.

ANDY SCAYSBROOK: That night as we returned to Coventry on the train was amazing. As I got into a cab the driver turned to me and said, 'I'm going nowhere mate, the streets are literally filled with people and you can't move, much better if you walk, sorry pal.' I started to see what he meant. The roads were crammed with cars sounding their horns and waving City scarves and flags from windows singing songs and generally going crazy. The night in the town centre was quite simply the most joyous gathering of people that I have ever been a part of. A whole city came out to party, united by the beautiful game, united by OUR football club. The city was alive like never before, this was our moment in the sunlight and the whole world was talking about our club, Coventry City.

ANDY TURNER: Back on the bus after exhausting the celebrations, an eerie silence fell among the fans as we slumped in our seats, reflecting on the sheer magnitude of what our unlikely lads had achieved. Home in Nuneaton we picked up bags of chips before heading for the George Eliot pub to sink a few pints and relive the magic to anyone who would listen.

BOB EALES: Not having been to a match during the cup run or even the season it was difficult to get tickets and I was condemned to watching the final on a portable black and white television in a bedsit in Plymouth. It was a fantastic feeling to see the guys go up to collect the cup, the hairs on the back of my neck standing up, who would have thought it, Coventry City had won the FA Cup! I may not have been there in body but I was certainly there in spirit.

STEVE & HEATHER TAYLOR: 'Go For It City' played its part on final day at Wembley. A lot of fans thought it sounded like a war cry at one point and that it helped Mabbutt's knee hit the ball into the net! In the night time back in Coventry it was all you heard, coming from club and pub doorways, people singing it in the streets at the top of their voices! The record reached number 61 in the UK charts, 35 in the independent chart. Gallup, who adjudicated the charts at the time and who, to add insult to injury were based in Tottenham, decided that Coventry City were picking up too many sales and, because the distributor figures didn't tally, they switched off all of the chart return machines in Coventry. They were apparently unaware that we were supplying the record shops and the sales were entirely genuine! The real position should have been at least top 30 and should have seen an appearance on *Top of the Pops* which sadly never materialised. It was, however, number one in Coventry for four weeks and was played incessantly on the radio and in establishments in and around the city for months afterwards.

It was an unbelievable experience, which produced something quite unique, and something to be extremely proud of. It is now folklore!

JOHN POYNTON: Steve Ogrizovic's wife had given birth to their daughter on the Thursday prior to the final so, when the buses went into Coventry on the Sunday, they went around Walsgrave Hospital so she could wave out the window. We eventually got to the Council House and, to be fair to Coventry City Council, they paid for it all with a great meal at the Hotel Leofric with expensive wine. I was then the only one to make a speech and it was a very memorable time.

STUART LINNELL: I had a call from the council to ask if I would host the Sunday in the city centre from the Council House balcony when the players arrived back. They were so late due to the huge crowds. Gary Newbon wanted first dibs for Central and the players and management took exception to the Council House being full of people they felt shouldn't have been there – family and friends of the council, freeloaders as they saw it. They did their bit, spoke to Gary Newbon, waved to the crowd, spoke to me and then left.

MIKE LIGGINS: The next day, being on the bus and coming down the Walsgrave Road, is implanted on my brain, seeing thousands upon thousands of people all the way into Coventry city centre. It was extraordinary. Mercia Sound carried the whole event live. It wasn't technically perfect but we captured the mood of excitement and pride in Coventry that day. I was on the media bus which travelled in front of the bus carrying the players. Everyone was so happy that the Sky Blues had actually won the cup, it was another 'pinch me' moment, a great memory and real privilege to have been there. Such happy days.

IAN WOODS: The following day was just as memorable as the final. I walked alongside the players' coach interviewing supporters who'd lined the route and then went back to the Council House for the civic party. I met Neil White who was working there for the *Birmingham Post*. We'd started the cup run as fans, jumping for joy at Old Trafford, and ended it as journalists reporting on an amazing win for Coventry City but, at heart, we were still supporters soaking up the best day of our lives.

NEIL WHITE: I was given the job of reporting from the Council House by the *Birmingham Post*. Standing on the balcony and touching the cup before John Sillett lifted it in front of tens of thousands of City supporters remains my best memory in a 30-year career in journalism. The next year I was married, our children became Junior Sky Blues and we have a cat called 'Oggy'.

IAN WOODS: I've been all over the world interviewing people over the years, incredibly famous people, and stories which are in the history books rather than just the newspapers but there is nothing that compares to that whole weekend of being with a team that had never won a major trophy before. There was something special about being with that team, I've been a journalist now for 30 years, have covered wars and disasters, interviewed Prime Ministers and American Presidents, but reporting for Mercia Sound on the Sky Blues' greatest ever day remains my favourite memory.

MIKE LIGGINS: I look back with incredible fondness to my time with Mercia. I was just so lucky that 1987 happened to be the cup run and I got to commentate on the FA Cup Final from the press box at Wembley Stadium.

STUART LINNELL: We produced the Mercia Sound car stickers with Carlton Dale, the operations director at Mercia Sound, they were everywhere! We wanted to associate it with the football club, the radio station and also put the Wembley logo on it. When it came back from the printers I thought, 'Perhaps we should have asked Wembley for permission!' The PR man at Wembley, Trevor Stephens, later to become a football agent, when I called him said they should have charged us for doing so but as we wouldn't be there again he said to just do it!

STEVE COCKRILL: I went with the youth team on the open-top bus. It was the right thing to do and we were, in 1987, only the third club ever to do the FA and Youth Cup double after Arsenal and Everton. I wasn't fit enough to play in the FA Youth Cup Final. I was eased back in gradually and didn't start playing again properly until the next season.

It was tough for me because I was part of the youth team but unable to play. Luckily for me John Sillett looked after me and it was a great time, I will never forget that. I also have a lot to thank Mick Kearns for, a fabulous man, along with Mick Coop. I've still got the tracksuit I wore on cup final day along with the red Coca-Cola t-shirt I wore in the Wembley pitch photograph where they spelt my surname as 'Cockerill' instead of 'Cockrill' on the posters produced after the game. I still wear a pair of Adidas Gazelles which I also wore on the day! I've also kept the hat that was thrown to me out of the crowd and have David

Phillips's shirt which he gave to me after the game – he wore a short-sleeved one for the final, I had his long-sleeved shirt with number two on the back. On the Wednesday after the game, Steve Evans from the *Coventry Evening Telegraph* interviewed me for an article which appeared under the banner 'The Mystery Man'. The photo caption read 'One of the gang: Steve Cockrill (back right) joins in the Wembley celebrations.'

STEVE EVANS: I remember speaking with Steve and his north-east accent. It was an enjoyable article to write.

IAN WINTER: The story of that fantastic final has been written into FA Cup folklore. Was it the best final ever? Probably. It was also a career highlight for me, commentating on an FA Cup Final.

STEVE LEE: I remember well the open-top bus journey from the Walsgrave Hospital area, Barry Davies commentated on it, I did the live interviews on the show titled *Coventry's Return* and the players were absolutely shattered. They'd been up until 3am. I was on the press bus and have never seen such an explosion of soccer passion for the city and its club. It was an astonishing outpouring, the whole programme had to be delayed because the bus was held up so many times. There were people dancing on the outside broadcast unit which threatened to put it off air! It was an amazing journalistic experience and one I'll always remember. In those days the FA Cup meant something, it was possibly bigger than winning the title. It has been devalued by the Premier League which has changed so many aspects of football.

One of the best football stories I covered at *Midlands Today* was the rise and rise of Coventry City. On the Monday after the final we had John Sillett in the studio and on the Tuesday I was completely knackered from the whole thing! I also did a piece on the final for *Football Focus*. It was great fun.

JENNY POOLE: In the weeks following the final hundreds of letters of congratulations arrived together with photographs of the players with the FA Cup to be autographed. At lunchtimes I would go into the cafeteria to put the photographs on the dining tables for the players to sign before they ate. It took some weeks but we got there in the end!

Vice-chairman Ted Stocker scooped £50,000 for his 50/1 bet on City back in September when he laid £1,000 on the Sky Blues to lift the trophy.

NEVILLE FOULGER: My match report was the last piece I filed for the *Coventry Evening Telegraph*:

Coventry Evening Telegraph, Monday 18 May 1987

By George, they did it!

Invincible City hit the jackpot

They came, they saw and they conquered. Brilliantly, gloriously but above all with style. Wembley, wonderful Wembley, became Coventry City's sunshine Shangri-La as the Sky Blue invasion swept all before it – including Tottenham Hotspur's multi-talented team of all stars.

Spurs had never been beaten in seven previous FA Cup finals. City had never even been to Wembley in their 104-year history. It looked an uneven contest – and it was. Poor Spurs didn't stand a chance. In those immortal words of Jimmy Hill, 'You can beat a team but you can't beat a team and a city.'

And on Saturday at the Mecca of English soccer the combination of Coventry City and the city of Coventry proved invincible. The bingo boys hit the jackpot. And they didn't just win the FA Cup – they won over a worldwide audience of millions who watched this classic confrontation. For make no mistake about it – this was one of the truly great finals. A game to be placed in Wembley's Hall of Fame. That alone represents a marvellous achievement and is a superb tribute to the team coached and motivated by Sky Blue 'old boys' George Curtis and John Sillett. And this was a team victory in every sense of the word.

Favourites Spurs might have had the Hoddles and Waddles, but the Sky Blues had what mattered most – passion, commitment, character, determination and a fierce will-to-win. Even going behind twice could not kill that. Like a dog with a bone the Sky Blues refused to let go of a dream. Dynamic midfield man Lloyd McGrath – my man of this marvellous match – typified City's spirit. Given the toughest job of anyone in this final – he had to mark the gifted Glenn Hoddle – the battling Brummie not only did that splendidly, he was also the man who created the Sky Blues' extra-time winner. Fed with an appetising pass down the unguarded right by substitute Graham Rodger in the 96th minute, non-stop McGrath chased it hungrily and then clipped across a centre clearly intended for City's advancing attackers. Spurs central defender Gary Mabbutt tried to intercept but in what must have been the cruellest moment of his career only succeeded in diverting the ball beyond a helpless Ray Clemence and into the roof of the net.

It was City's cup and, at that moment, even Spurs accepted it. Their heads dropped, their spirits wilted and the greatest battle the Sky Blues have ever waged was over. Spurs had nothing left to give and only a great save from Clemence off Michael Gynn and a missed opportunity from the dazzling Dave Bennett prevented City making it the 'Old Five'. It was one of the great team triumphs in cup final history. Even the shuffle caused by the tragic injury to Brian Borrows failed to ruffle or disturb City.

Dave Phillips took over at right-back as though he never played anywhere else and while he would be kicking himself that he did not score a couple of goals, Gynn's pace and willingness to run at the defence made him a constant thorn in Spurs' side. McGrath's grip on Hoddle and Nick Pickering's readiness to work and run as hard as his opposite number Paul Allen always gave the Sky Blues a firm foothold in the area of the pitch Spurs believed they would dominate – midfield.

In the end Spurs had to accept the unpalatable fact that their best moment was the second minute of the match when Clive Allen headed a stunning opening goal from Waddle's centre. Picking the ball out of the net was Steve Ogrizovic's first touch and half the City side had not been anywhere near the ball. Such a disastrous start might have finished off many teams – but not the 1987 Sky Blues model. It needs more than an early goal to bother them – by George and John it does!

By the ninth minute they were level as 'Benno' proved yet again his love of the big occasion with a razor sharp strike after a perfect headed flick-on from Keith Houchen. For the next half-an-hour City produced some quality football and yet still found themselves 2-1 down at half-time. A 42nd-minute free kick from the right left Oggy in no-man's land

and as Brian Kilcline and Mabbutt made contact with the ball at virtually the same moment it flew into the net. It looked an own goal but Mabbutt claimed it and Kilcline was happy to allow him to do so. The second half belonged to City and Houchen's spectacular flying headed equaliser from Bennett's cross in the 63rd minute saw justice done. That was 'Roy of the Rovers' Houchen's fifth goal in the FA Cup. His fairytale story this season is enough to have you believing in Santa Claus again.

Once the game had gone into extra time it was always going to be City's cup – even though skipper Kilcline had to miss the final 30 minutes because of injury. But Rodger proved an heroic deputy and his pass to McGrath for that all important goal must surely be the finest moment of his career. On such a day, though, it seems churlish to single out individuals. Every City player was a hero and it was just McGrath's amazing energy in extra time which swung the man of the match vote his way.

One thing is for sure – these super Sky Blues will now have the biggest fan club in their history. It will spread across the world.

The summer of 1987 saw David Speedie signed from Chelsea for £780,000 with Ian Painter and Paul Culpin leaving the club. League champions Everton were City's opponents in the Charity Shield when a Wayne Clarke goal gave the Toffees victory in front of 88,000 at Wembley. Brian Borrows and Steve Sedgley made substitute appearances during the game. The Sky Blues would finish the season once again in tenth position with an average crowd at Highfield Road of 17,530. Cyrille Regis was recalled to the England squad and was top scorer with 12 goals in all competitions.

As the FA Cup was won during the five-year European ban on English clubs the Sky Blues were unable to take their place in the European Cup Winners' Cup. Their hold on the FA Cup was relinquished at Highfield Road in round four as Watford won 1-0 in front of 22,000 supporters. Steve Cockrill was present at Highfield Road for the Torquay tie but had returned to fitness by the time Watford visited and was not in the stands to see City bow out. The 'Crazy Gang' of Wimbledon, managed by Bobby Gould, assisted by Don Howe and with Terry Gibson in their line-up, upset the form book in the final with a 1-0 win over Liverpool.

Steve Ogrizovic went on to play in City's colours for a further 13 seasons, becoming the club's leading appearance maker of all time: 601 games and one goal. He is still with the club in the capacity of goalkeeping coach after originally joining for £72,500 in the summer of 1984 from Shrewsbury Town.

Brian Borrows made 488 first-team appearances, the fourth-highest in the history of the club, before leaving to join Swindon Town in the summer of 1997. After two seasons at the County Ground he retired from playing and has since coached the Academy sides at Coventry and Derby County. Brian is now a regional coach for the PFA in the Midlands.

Greg Downs joined Birmingham City in the summer of 1990. He then moved on after a season to join Hereford United, managed by John Sillett. Greg succeeded Sillett after 12 months and took on the role of player-manager for a further two years. In 1995 he joined the police force in Norfolk where he remains to this day.

Lloyd McGrath played in Sky Blue until the summer of 1994 and made 258 starts for the club. He moved to Portsmouth for two seasons before a spell in Hong Kong and retirement in 1997. Lloyd now owns the popular Hawkes Mill Sports Club in Coventry.

Brian Kilcline was sold by Terry Butcher in 1991 to Oldham Athletic after 213 appearances and 35 goals. After Oldham he was signed by Kevin Keegan to save Newcastle from relegation to the third tier prior to the revolution under the former Liverpool man. After a spell with Swindon Town during their sole Premier League campaign he moved to Mansfield then secured promotion from the Conference for Halifax Town prior to retirement.

He now shares his time between the UK and Portugal and has worked for many years in property development.

Trevor Peake was also sold by Terry Butcher, to Luton Town in August 1991, where he stayed until the Sky Blues asked him to return in a coaching capacity in 1998. He stayed until 2003 when he moved to work with Leicester City's academy where he remains to this day. His 334 appearances for the Sky Blues see him lie 11th in the all-time appearance list.

Dave Bennett departed for Sheffield Wednesday in the spring of 1989 after suffering a broken leg in a collision with Derby's Peter Shilton just ten months after the cup win. After 209 appearances and 35 goals in Sky Blue he also played for Swindon Town and Shrewsbury Town where he suffered further broken legs prior to retirement in 1992. He returned to Highfield Road when he came on as substitute for Wednesday in their 4-1 victory in March 1990 and the stadium rose as one.

David Phillips departed Highfield Road in the summer of 1989 after three seasons with the club to become Norwich City's record signing for a fee of £550,000. After four seasons at Carrow Road he spent a similar amount of time at Nottingham Forest where he was part of the team, post-Brian Clough, that secured promotion back to the Premier League. David also played for Huddersfield, Lincoln and Stevenage before retirement in 2001. He now works for Sky Sports as part of its La Liga commentary team.

Michael Gynn stayed for many years after Wembley and left for Stoke City in the summer of 1993 after 291 appearances and ten seasons in Sky Blue. He retired in 1995 and, to this day, works for Royal Mail and as a football analyst for the PFA, Press Association and Opta.

Cyrille Regis was released by Terry Butcher in the summer of 1991 after 281 appearances and 62 goals. He reunited with Ron Atkinson at Aston Villa and won a league runners-up medal in the first season of the Premier League, 1992/93, when Villa were pipped to the title by Manchester United. Cyrille also played for Wolves, Wycombe and Chester before retirement in 1996. He now works for the Stellar Football agency as a football agent.

Keith Houchen departed for Hibernian in March 1989 after 66 appearances, scoring 12 goals, five of which came during the cup run. Keith also played for Port Vale and Hartlepool including a spell as player-manager in 1995 before he retired from the game in 1996. He has since set up student accommodation with a local university and collates statistics on York City, Bradford City and Leeds United for Opta having previously worked for the Press Association.

Nick Pickering spent only one more season at Highfield Road before leaving in the summer of 1988 for Derby County. He played 94 times for City and scored ten goals during his time at the club. After three years at the Baseball Ground he moved on to Darlington and Burnley before retiring with a foot injury at the age of 31 in 1994. He moved back home to Sunderland and worked for seven years commentating on their matches for BBC Radio

Newcastle. Nick now runs football holiday courses and after-school football clubs. During his career he had been a part of the England under-21 side that won the 1984 European Championship tournament and also played in the 1985 Milk Cup Final for Sunderland against Norwich City in a game refereed by one Neil Midgley.

Dean Emerson left City for Hartlepool in the summer of 1991 after 132 appearances for the club. It was his pass in August 1989 that set up a goal for David Smith in a 2-1 win over Manchester City to take the Sky Blues top of the First Division for the first time ever. Dean still lives in the city and is often seen at the Ricoh Arena with the Former Players' Association.

Steve Sedgley transferred to Tottenham for £750,000 in the summer of 1989 after 103 appearances in Sky Blue. He added to his FA Cup medal haul in 1991 when Spurs beat Nottingham Forest 2-1, a game dominated by Paul Gascoigne's knee injury as a result of a reckless tackle. Steve spent five seasons at White Hart Lane before three seasons apiece at Ipswich and Wolves before retirement in 2000 aged 32. After a spell in charge of Kingstonian and coaching at Luton he now runs his own construction company in St Albans.

Graham Rodger signed for Luton Town in the summer of 1989 after 43 appearances for City. He spent three seasons at Kenilworth Road before moving to Grimsby Town where he spent six seasons before retiring in 1998. Graham has taken on a number of roles at Blundell Park, including manager, and is currently community manager, working with former Sky Blue David Smith who is the club's commercial manager.

Paul Culpin departed Highfield Road after two seasons in the summer of 1987 when he rejoined former Nuneaton Borough boss Graham Carr at all-conquering Northampton Town. After two seasons with the Cobblers and further spells with Peterborough and Hereford, he returned to Manor Park in 1992. Paul's tally of 55 goals in all competitions (41 in the league) in 1983/84 remains a Conference seasonal record to this day. While at Highfield Road, Paul scored on his debut at Villa Park in a 1-1 draw and played nine times in total, adding a further strike to his name.

Steve Cockrill left City in 1989 and returned to his native Hartlepool where he signed for Spennymoor United for four years and also turned out for York City and Hartlepool's reserve teams in the Central League. At the same time he gained his building qualifications and has run a building company for the last 12 years with a business partner. Steve is also chairman of Seaton Carew Football Club where his young son plays and is a level two coach looking to do his UEFA B Licence through the PFA.

John Sillett stepped up from the role of chief coach to replace George Curtis as manager in the summer of 1987 and remained in the role until November 1990. In the year of the cup run he, along with George Curtis, led the side to a tenth-place finish. This was repeated in 1987/88 and improved upon in 1988/89 when they finished in seventh position, the club's highest finish for 11 years. With 13 games to play the side sat in third position. His final full season in charge saw City top the First Division for the first time ever after four games and they went on to finish 12th.

George Curtis returned to his role of managing director in the summer of 1987. The man who had captained Jimmy Hill's side from the Fourth Division to the First Division in the mid-60s stepped down after sharing with Sillett the greatest moment in the club's history.

John Poynton remained chairman until 1991 after taking charge in the summer of 1983. He now lives back in Jersey where he is the business manager for Jersey Rugby Club.

George Dalton's final season with the first team was 1997/98. He then went on to work with the club's academy for a year before taking early retirement and moved back home to Newcastle. George had joined the club, under Gordon Milne and Ron Wylie, in 1976.

Terry Gibson played for Manchester United until the summer of 1987 when he joined Bobby Gould at Wimbledon. He also played for Swindon, Peterborough and Barnet before moving into management alongside Ray Clemence at Barnet. Terry also assisted Lawrie Sanchez with Northern Ireland, Wycombe Wanderers and Fulham and now works with David Phillips as a co-commentator for Sky Sports La Liga coverage.

Micky Adams moved from Leeds to Southampton in 1989 and spent five seasons back in the top flight. He began his management career at Fulham in 1996 and returned to the Sky Blues for two seasons in 2005 when they moved to the Ricoh Arena. Micky has since managed

Leicester, Brighton, Sheffield United, Port Vale and Tranmere Rovers.

Graham Hover left the club in 2005 after 21 years as club secretary. He spent a brief time at Gillingham and now works as a match delegate for UEFA.

Neville Foulger left the *Coventry Evening Telegraph* after the cup final and took up a job in Leicester running a freelance agency sports section for a few years called Leicester News Service. He then set up on his own and worked for BBC Radio Leicester from the early 1990s until 2005, commentating on Leicester City and also covering Leicestershire in cricket's County Championship. Ten years ago the *Leicester Mercury* asked Neville to write a weekly column on a freelance basis commenting on Leicester City while the Press Association asked him to cover the cricket until September 2014 when he finally retired at the age of 75.

Steve Evans replaced Neville Foulger and covered the Sky Blues until 1990 when he left the sports desk and returned to general news reporting and feature writing. He moved to the paper's Nuneaton office where he led a small news team covering north Warwickshire. Steve took early retirement in 2007 after 36 years with the *Coventry Evening Telegraph*. He is still involved with journalism as a correspondent for the Press Association and ITN, usually at General Election time.

Mike Liggins left Mercia Sound in September 1987. Mercia supplied a news service to Coventry Cable TV and TV experience was gained by the newsroom. Mike went to the BBC's *Look East* in Norwich where he remains to this day.

Ian Woods left Mercia Sound in December 1987 to join the BBC in Nottingham as a reporter with *Midlands Today* before, in 1991, moving to *East Midlands Today* for four years as presenter. He joined Sky News in 1995 as sports correspondent, then as sports editor and returned to news reporting in 2000. Ian is now senior news correspondent, still has his Sky Blues season ticket and attends matches with Neil White.

Rob Gurney became the Sky Blues matchday commentator between 1989 and 2001 before moving to Radio WM where he remains to this day. He still watches the Sky Blues, work commitments permitting, and was one of the most popular commentators in recent times with the City faithful.

Stuart Linnell continued for some years running Mercia – as managing director and programme controller. With various radio station mergers he held both of those roles at Leicester Sound as well for a time. A number of different mergers and combination of stations within corporate groupings followed until he went back into regular, front-line broadcasting working for BBC WM, BBC TV, BBC Radio 5 Live, Sky Sports News, Today FM, Setanta Sports, Talk Sport, BBC Radio Derby, BBC Hereford and Worcester, BBC Coventry and Warwickshire and BBC Radio Northampton. These days, he presents the weekday breakfast show for BBC Radio Northampton along with sports and occasional other shows for BBC Coventry and Warwickshire.

Ian Bolton left Mercia Sound in March 1987 and joined Radio WM where he stayed for two years before moving to BBC Radio Sport in London. From 1991 to 94 Ian was a TV sports presenter at *East Midlands Today* before he joined Sky Sports in 1994 as a presenter/reporter where he remains to this day. He is currently a senior reporter at Sky Sports News HQ.

Ian Winter spent ten years at Radio WM before he moved to Norwich in 1996 with *Look East* as a TV sports reporter/presenter. In 2006 he returned in a similar role to *Midlands Today* where he remains to this day.

Steve Lee moved from *Midlands Today* to BBC Sport and covered the 1998 World Cup. He joined Sky Sports, for whom he still works, and also worked for Channel 4 on its cricket coverage and Channel 5's football. Steve is still freelancing now and working towards a degree in history.

Bob Hall continued to freelance for ITV until 2009. He qualified as a teacher and taught Media Studies in college until January of this year when he left to become head of news and sport for the new local television channel serving the West Midlands – Big Centre TV. Bob continues to broadcast for Sky Sports as well as hosting dinners and events.

Gary Newbon presents *Time of Their Lives* on Sky Sports. He worked for ITV for 36 years and covered seven football

World Cups for the channel during this time. Gary also presented phone-in show *You're on Sky Sports.*

Alan Biggs has broadcast nationally as a match reporter for the BBC since 1989 and written for many national newspapers. He has written *Confessions of a Football Reporter* and is also a match reporter for talkSPORT and Sky Sports.

Andy Scaysbrook left Coventry in the summer of 1987 and spent seven years with the *Bournemouth Evening Echo* as a staff photographer then moved to the *Southampton Echo* for four years on the picture desk. He then resumed his freelance photography and worked for the *Sunday Times*, *Observer* and *Daily Telegraph.* Andy now spends his time teaching and training photographers and runs workshops around the world. You can view his work at www.andyscaysbrook.com.

Steve and **Heather Taylor** continue to write and produce music, achieving their first major cover in 1989 when Shakin' Stevens asked them to produce 'Love Attack' which reached number 28 in the charts. Steve played on the track and sang backing vocals on *Top of the Pops.* The 1990s were spent writing and recording people in the studio, including Dave Willetts and Daniel O'Donnell whom they had two hit singles with in 1996. 'Footsteps' has now sold over a million copies. They had further success with Daniel in 1997 and 1998 while in 1999 three of their songs appeared on his *Greatest Hits* album. The millennium saw a period of talent development and Steve doing live shows (*In Dreams, The Voice of Roy Orbison, Rockin on Heaven's Door* and their own show, *Steve Taylor's Buddy Holly Rock 'n' Roll*

Party. Steve and Heather wrote 'We'll Say Goodbye'to mark the end of the Highfield Road era and 'Come on, Come on' to mark the opening of the Ricoh Arena. In 2013 they were inducted on to the Coventry Wall of Fame and also form part of the exhibition in the Coventry Music Museum.

Andy Turner graduated from Leeds University in 1989 and joined the *Evening Tribune* newspaper, in Nuneaton, then the smallest regional evening paper in the country. He switched to the *Coventry Telegraph* in January 1992 and was appointed Sky Blues reporter in early 1998. The first match Andy covered was the FA Cup third round tie at Liverpool when the Sky Blues won 3-1, just one week after the Darren Huckerby-inspired 3-2 victory over Manchester United at Highfield Road.

Geoff Foster joined the BBC in 1993 to cover sport in Coventry and Warwickshire. He commentates on all sports including Sky Blues matches and is a popular voice on the local airwaves to this day.

Jim Brown became club historian and statistician in March 1994 and has a weekly column in the *Coventry Telegraph*. In 2006 he played a major part in launching the Coventry City Former Players' Association in his role of chairman.

Jenny Poole stayed at the club until 2010. In her role as secretary the last manager she worked for was Chris Coleman.

Neil White is now the editor of the *Derby Telegraph*. He attends City matches with long-time friend Ian Woods.

Mike Young is now the membership secretary of the Coventry City Former Players' Association.

Frank Pritchard became the voice of Coventry City Clubcall during the 1993/94 season. He was a freelance broadcaster for 33 years until 2005 which included four years on ITV's *Goal Rush* programme. Prior to the cup run he was the club's first ever DJ at Highfield Road and did this for two seasons in the 1960s. He is now an integral part of the Former Players' Association committee.

Dean Nelson and **Bob Eales** are committee members of the Coventry City Former Players' Association and can be found at the Ricoh on matchdays.

Kev Monks is present at every City game and is editor of the Covsupport News Service (www.coventrycity-mad.co.uk)

Lee Corden now works for Coventry-based media agency Advent Communications on behalf of a range of companies and organisations including Coventry City Football Club. He writes copy for the club programme and can be seen either in the press box on matchdays or in the Family Stand with his two sons, Joseph and Joshua, and dad John, with whom he attended every round of the cup run in 1987.

Matt Partridge, Matt Kerr, Blake Waugh, Calvin Urquhart, Danny Finlay, Gavin Clifton, Neil Jones and **Rob Summerfield** are all still regulars at the Ricoh Arena as is **Moz Baker**, who is part of the Sky Blue Trust board, responsible for press, public relations and events.

Wembley match referee Neil Midgley sadly passed away in 2001. In April 1988 he refereed the visit of Charlton Athletic to Highfield Road. As the game began, 'One Neil Midgley, there's only one Neil Midgley' rang out from the West Terrace in tribute to the man who played his part in ensuring the 1987 FA Cup Final was one of the best ever seen at Wembley stadium.